Generational Restoration

The Significance of Generational Influences

They will rebuild the ancient ruins
and restore the places long devastated;
they will renew the ruined cities
that have been devastated for generations.
Isaiah 61:4[NIV]

Robert John Morrissette

Generational Restoration
Author: Robert John Morrissette
ISBN: 978-0976354970
Library of Congress Control Number: 2014921794

Publisher
Big Blue Skies of Idaho LLC
Coeur d'Alene, Idaho 83815
United States of America

Bible Versions Information
New International Version® (NIV) Copyright ©1973 by International Bible Society
New American Standard Bible® Copyright © 1995 by The Lockman Foundation
The Message (MSG) Copyright © 2002
King James Version (KJV) No copyright: public domain

Edited by: John, Mark and Jonah Sandford (3 generations!)
Cover Design and Layout by: Robert John Morrissette. All images are personal property or public domain.
Printed by: CreateSpace, Charleston, SC, USA

Unless otherwise stated, all verses quoted throughout this book are from the New American Standard Bible.

Note: As appropriate, names and other identifying information used throughout this book as illustrations have been changed to protect privacy.

May the Lord use you mightily
to remove the influence of generational iniquities
so that you and your descendants may be blessed.

And...
May your descendants be blessed
by the sacrifices you make,
by the trials you endure,
by the obstacles you overcome,
and by the character you build.

Now to Him who is able to do far more abundantly beyond
all that we ask or think, according to the power that
works within us, to Him be the glory in the church and in
Christ Jesus to all generations forever and ever. Amen.
Ephesians 3:20

About the Author

Rob's experiences include being a prayer minister, professional counselor, software engineer, automotive R&D technician, author, publisher, teacher, and speaker. Rob's desire is for others to experience the Father's love.

For information about prayer ministry...

elijah house
healing hearts. changing lives.

Elijah House is an international Christian prayer-ministry organization with locations throughout the world.

Elijah House provides:
- Teaching and training: schools and seminars
- Resources: books, DVDs and CDs
- Prayer ministry and internships

To locate an Elijah House near you...
Go to: ElijahHouse.org

Scan code below to go to website.

Other books by Rob Morrissette

Pray Through It: How to identify and resolve problems that are rooted in unresolved issues from your past. This book contains applications and many encouraging stories of those who experienced change. ISBN: 978-0976354963 Also available in Spanish (*Oraciòn que toca las racìces* (ISBN: 978-0976354918), as well as in Japanese and Finnish.

Hey God, Are We There Yet?: The rewards of waiting on God! Learn about God's divine purposes in waiting and what to do while waiting. Included in the book is a 40-day devotional. Know that God has good things in store for you. And that He is worth the wait! ISBN: 978-0976354949

Table of Content

**God is good,
All the time!**

Introduction

his book is the result of a personal journey – a journey of seeking freedom from, and healing for, various recurring issues. Such troubling issues weren't only in my life, but also in the lives of others – others who were determined to no longer accommodate or ignore such issues. We wanted resolution and change. Along this journey, I discovered biblical principles that, when applied, brought about the change we were seeking. As for this book, its primary focus is about the significance of unresolved generational issues, and how to identify and address them.

The insights and principles shared in this book are ones I have found to be tremendously helpful. Yet they are not cure-alls. In other words, not all recurring problems are because of generational issues. Just like the tools in a toolbox, each tool has a specific application. A hammer is used for driving and removing nails. A screwdriver is useful for its purposes, but not for nails. So, whenever generational issues are involved, the tools are applicable for addressing them and have certainly been proven effective.

Concerning generational iniquities, the enemy's goal is to keep us ignorant about them and how they impact our lives, keeping you and your family line in bondage. But once we know how to identify and properly deal with generational iniquities, this will make a tremendous difference in ours lives and that of others. For once set free, restoration begins to occur in the generations, re-establishing God's intended purposes for your family line and blessing the generations to come.

My prayer is that this book will be a blessing to you. That it will assist you in resolving any problems that are related to unresolved generational issues. That it will also be useful in providing insight as you minister to others. And, even more so, that you will stand out amidst your family line as one who made a difference, who brought about generational

1

reconciliation and thus passed blessing on to subsequent generations.

Contained within this book are some wonderful stories of those who experienced change after identifying generational root causes and praying through them. These stories are included for your encouragement and to testify of the amazing redemptive grace of our Lord Jesus Christ!

Concerning such things...

... which we have heard and known,
And our fathers have told us.
We will not conceal them from their children,
But tell to the generation to come the praises of the Lord,
And His strength and His wondrous works that He has done.
Psalms 78:3-4

Generational Issues

We acknowledge, O LORD, our wickedness,
and the iniquity of our fathers:
for we have sinned against Thee.
Jeremiah 14:20 KJV

Poor and Miserable

ears ago, I was in England, where I had been invited to speak at a conference. During the worship time, I had a startling experience. A few minutes before I was to be introduced to speak, the Lord spoke to me in my mind. He said, "Your father was supposed to be here." This came as quite a surprise. For at that moment, I wasn't trying to hear God but rather I was busy thinking about the message I was about to share. But also, I was confused, for I didn't understand what the Lord meant.

So I asked the Lord, "What do you mean, my father was supposed to be here?" Again He said, "Your father was supposed to be here." Still not understanding, I asked, "Do you mean that he was supposed to speak today at this conference, and not me?" Once more the Lord said, "Your father was supposed to be here." So I said, "I don't understand. What do you mean?" Then the Lord began to explain to me what He meant.

He told me that, many years before I was born, He had approached my father while he was in college. The Lord wanted my father to include Him in whatever he pursued. God also had some specific tasks He wanted my father to accomplish in his life. For one, if my father had chosen to obey God, he would have ended up ministering to people and doing speaking engagements, not unlike what I was doing.

When the Lord had approached my father, my father struggled with what was being asked of him. He knew that

3

following Jesus was the right thing to do, but there was an objection in his heart. For some reason, he thought that, if he were to do what God wanted, he would be poor and miserable. And, in so doing, he wouldn't be able to do what he wanted. So, instead of challenging these thoughts, he gave in to them. He didn't even bother to share his struggle with the Lord, and thus ask for help. Instead, he decided to live life as he wanted. Ironically, God wasn't asking my father not to pursue his own interests and goals. Rather, God only wanted my father to include His leading in all that he did. He also wanted to help my father overcome this wrong way of thinking.

So, I asked the Lord, "Why did my father think this way?"

The Lord indicated that my father's resentments towards his father had caused him to have a wrong perspective. My grandfather and my father didn't have a close relationship. Their relationship was utilitarian and distant. My father saw him as harsh and only concerned about whether the chores were done. As a child, my father felt that his father wasn't interested in any of his interests, such as having adventures and enjoying life. This tempted my father to resent my grandfather. And as a result, it wrote on my father's heart, "If you do what your father wants, even though it is the right thing to do, it won't be fun – and you will be poor and miserable." As result, my father projected his resentment of his father toward God, rather than confronting it.

Then God added something. He said, "Your grandfather did the same thing."

Wow! Here, in a short time, I had found out that there were two previous generations of men in my family who turned away from God's direction in their life. And they did so out of the belief, "If I do God's will, I will be poor and miserable." And ironically, this very theme was something I had struggled with for many years!

So with this new information, I began to pray. And as I did, I found myself saying things like, "Forgive us…" and, "We have sinned…" These words just welled-up from within my spirit. As I prayed, I confessed the resentment my father had toward his father, as well as that which my grandfather had

4

toward his father. Concerning both of them, I confessed their choice to believe, "If we follow God, we will be poor and miserable." I acknowledged how they chose to live their lives, excluding God's input and direction by giving in to a lie instead of challenging it, thereby questioning God's goodness. As a result, they skewed their view of God, believing that He wouldn't consider their welfare in His will for them. I also acknowledged their unwillingness to confront their fears and to ask God for help. Lastly, I confessed how I had believed the same lie they had.

During this time of prayer, I found myself crying, feeling great sorrow and loss. And when I had finished praying, I was then introduced to speak.

As I was being introduced, something was different. For the first time in my life, I was free of a way of thinking with which I have struggled throughout my life. I could literally feel that it was gone. It had lifted off of me. It was no longer lurking somewhere in the back of my mind. For, up until that time, on some level I was aware of this wrong way of thinking, but the best I could do was to resist and reject it. Though these efforts did help, it would never completely make the thoughts go away. But, now, I was free!

Some time afterwards, my mother shared with me several things that confirmed what the Lord had revealed to me about my father were true. This was encouraging.

Prior to this time, whenever I struggled financially or went through a difficult time period, negative thoughts would come to mind. Thoughts like, "This experience (being poor or miserable) is happening because I am a Christian!" And with them often came an edge of bitterness in my heart. I would find myself questioning God's character, as if He wasn't good. Sometimes I felt as if God didn't care. It felt as if all He wanted was for me to do His will, while He had no interest in my desires or my needs. It seemed as though His only concern was that I complete the assignments He gave me to do - just as my fore-fathers had believed.

When I was a child, I remember missionaries visiting our church. They would give a talk and share about their

5

experiences and the wonderful things God was doing. But I tended to focus on their outdated clothes, their difficult circumstances, and their ongoing need for financial support. I thought, "Who would want to be a missionary?!" I also remember being afraid that God might someday require me to be a missionary. In my mind, as a child, this only reinforced the thought that "if I serve God, I will be poor and miserable."

Looking back, I realize that what I failed to see was that these missionaries loved what they were doing. They didn't care that their clothes were outdated. All they cared about was getting back on the mission field to minister and love people to Jesus. They were inviting us to participate in their adventure with Jesus as missionaries by supporting them. Though all this was right in front of me, the generational lie of "poor and miserable" blinded me, causing me to focus on the wrong things.

As a young man, I wrestled in my heart with the same erroneous beliefs as my forefathers. Though the Bible has a lot to say about joy, prosperity, and blessing, these seemed to not apply to my life. What the Bible says about sufferings, trials, and difficult times, my heart tended to focus on these topics instead. Therefore, should I not expect such things as a normal part of life? And are they not to be paired with such virtues as perseverance, endurance, and faith? Yet, I found myself often gravitating toward the books of Job and Ecclesiastes, as well as other passages in the Bible that speak of suffering and trials. My view of life was out of balance.

Over time, I began to recognize the imbalance in my thinking. For the Bible definitely speaks of times of prosperity and blessing as well. In addition, we are told to learn to be peaceful and contented despite our circumstances. So, I began to dwell upon these thoughts and to seek ways to put them into practice. This definitely helped, giving me some measure of success. Yet, it didn't completely get rid of the struggle. Despite my efforts to console myself with various passages, I still struggled to experience the peace and contentment the Bible says I should have despite my circumstances.

All it took was for me to have my guard down and for some difficult situation to occur, and the old way of thinking would come back again. Then I would find myself spending a lot of time trying to recover. The only recourse was to confess my sin of believing such lies, tell myself the truth, and put the truth into practice again. This required a lot of maintenance. Besides, there was nothing better that I knew to do.

But after confessing the generational iniquities of my father and grandfather, this all changed. Now, whenever I have financially and go through hard times, I no longer struggle with the old lies. Instead, I see alternatives to my situation, have peace despite my circumstances, and am able to believe that God is in control and has a plan.

Out of this experience came several profound realizations.

For one, this experience made me realize just how much of an impact unresolved generational issues can have. Who would have thought that something done by someone else in the past could have had such an impact on my own life?! And I wasn't even alive when these events took place! Even more profound is that I never knew about these events, and yet they had an impact upon me. They were hidden decisions that my father and his father had both committed separately. They had never told anyone.

This realization only reinforced the fact that all sin, whether hidden or not, does affect others. In this case, it affected my family line. Is it any wonder why it's so important that we confess our sins?! Thinking that our hidden sins are private, and therefore affect no one else, is one of the many deceptions of sin.

I would never have considered that some of the very thoughts with which I had been struggling weren't even my own. Since I had no knowledge of their source, I just assumed that they were mine. But once the source was identified and acknowledged through confession in prayer, they left.

This brings up another profound realization: not everything we think or feel is necessarily our own thoughts and feelings.

In most instances, the thoughts and feelings we experience are our own. But sometimes they are from other sources. Without knowing this, we might assume they are our own and thus make bad decisions or react based upon them despite our ignorance.

These extraneous thoughts and feelings can come from several sources. They can be from natural sources, such as lack of sleep, something we ate that didn't agree with us, or even an illness. They can be from something in our environment, such as a chemical or strong odor. Drugs can also have this effect.

It can simply be that one has been feeding one's sinful inclinations. Or, such thoughts could also be from a spiritual source, such as an oppression or attack from a demon. The enemy does this to tempt us to make these negative thoughts our own and thus give in to sin.

Sometimes God will allow us to feel the pains or struggles of others so we can pray empathically for them with understanding. Those who do intercession are very familiar with this.

But also, unresolved generational issues are another source to consider. As in my story, I was being influenced by thoughts that weren't even my own.

Knowing that there are other explanations for some of the thoughts and feelings we experience is very helpful. At the same time, we must never let this become an excuse for sinful behaviors, actions and attitudes. Each of us is responsible for how we choose to respond to whatever thoughts and feelings we experience despite regardless of the source.

Another profound realization is that, by properly dealing with generational issues in prayer, it removes their power of influence. So it was for me concerning my father and grandfather. I no longer struggle with the decisions they had made. These no longer invade my thinking. This isn't to say that I am free from temptation. Rather, there is one less thing influencing me to think or act wrongly about God and my life.

This experience demonstrated to me that the Lord can reveal to hidden, unresolved historical events that I would not have known otherwise. This only makes sense since He knows all things!

But perhaps the most important thing is that God has a remedy for ridding the impact of negative generational events and thus freeing us and future generations to come!

Things to Consider

- What has been some of your previous thinking about why you struggle with ongoing unresolved issues?
- What are some of your thoughts on the possibility of the impact of unresolved generational issues?
- What are some experiences in which you have struggled with feelings or thoughts that you have had to repeatedly resist?

Dealing with Personal Root Causes

Search me, O God, and know my heart;
Try me and know my anxious thoughts;
And see if there be any hurtful way in me,
And lead me in the everlasting way.
Psalms 139:23-24

No Support

O ver the years, Cathy had been diligent to work through many of her personal issues. During this process, she had come to recognize that certain negative behaviors and thought patterns in her adult life had originated in her childhood. This insight was an amazing realization for her. She could finally see the similarities between her present behaviors and her childhood experiences. These experiences had tempted her to hold resentment toward those who hurt her. In addition, she had made negative decisions in her heart. Even though years had gone by, and she could no longer feel the resentment, the bad fruit of those experiences had become evident in her life.

But upon identifying and praying through specific experiences, Cathy found much relief and change in her life. She found this to be very encouraging, especially since so many other things she had tried before had helped very little, or not at all. She now understood just how much of an impact unresolved past experiences can have later on in one's life.

For example, some of the communication issues Cathy had with her husband were similar to those she had with her parents. And when she prayed through those childhood experiences, the dynamics in her marriage began to change. As she applied this to other areas of her life, she found healing as well.

Though these changes did make a beneficial difference in Cathy's life, in some areas change remained incomplete. One such area was in her relationship with authority figures. This puzzled her. She wondered why she was experiencing freedom in some ways but not in other ways despite all she had done. Had she missed something?

Because of Cathy's skills as a counselor and teacher, she was given many opportunities. In addition, those in authority would show an interest and give her verbal support. But, when times came when she needed their support in action, all too often they wouldn't exercise any authority on her behalf.

For instance, when lies began to spread about Cathy, those in leadership did nothing to silence or refute them. Even when she appealed to authority figures, hoping they would do something, they did nothing. Though they sometimes acknowledged what had happened and agreed with her, they didn't do anything to defend her.

Though this was a pattern in Cathy's life, she did not know how to stop it. She felt that all she could do was to make the best of it. She did this by trying to continue honoring and pursuing relationships with those in authority, despite the ongoing hurtful experiences and her frustrations with them. This took a lot of effort on her part to not give up, but she didn't know what else to do.

There was one thing that Cathy had done that was very helpful. She had made a list of the negative messages she had felt during her hurtful experiences with authority figures. This list included things like: "No one will listen to me," "They won't understand my heart," "Others won't be helpful," and, "They will listen to someone else but not to me." Concerning her own personal history, she had prayed through her list, renouncing her decisions and forgiving those who had offended her. So because there was still bad fruit in her life, this was a good indicator that could still be some other possible root causes.

So, we asked the Lord for more insight. He indicated that Cathy's experiences were related to unresolved generational issues. As she listened, the Lord revealed to her mind what had happened.

A young man (an ancestor of Cathy's) was the son of a prominent man who had influence and power. This son had fallen in love with a young woman. And, despite the fact that she was a prostitute, he loved her very much and saw her potential. He saw her for who she really was, realizing that she had become a prostitute because of all the hurt and abuse she had endured while growing up.

The young man went to his father, wanting to obtain approval and support to marry the woman he loved. But unfortunately his father became very upset, showing no understanding. In an attempt to try to deter his son from his decision, the father did a very insensitive thing. He shamed his son publicly in front of everyone in the town. He also threatened his son by saying, "I will disinherit you. You are no longer my son!"

The father was only concerned about his reputation. He knew that his son would one day inherit his place of influence. If his son married this woman, the father feared how it would reflect upon his reputation. He was overly concerned with appearances and was unwilling to see his son's heart. This blinded him to the fact that he could have used his position of influence to help and bless his son, showing support and ministering to the woman his son loved (the Lord only knows what blessing would have come if the father hadn't given in to the fear of man).

Because of his position of influence, when he had shamed his son, many of the townspeople took the father's side. They heckled and cursed the young man. Soon, lies began to circulate, but the father did nothing to stop them. Despite this, there were some who didn't agree with what was happening. They seemed to have understood the young man's intentions and what was in his heart. And, perhaps, they could have done something that would have helped to rescue the young man. This, in turn, would have helped the woman as well. But instead, they did nothing. Consequently, they were just as guilty and unsupportive for being silent.

As a result, the young man and his desired wife-to-be became resentful and bitter. The young man vowed never to forgive his father. He also pledged to do whatever he could to shame his father. Out of hurt and tremendous bitterness, the woman cursed the young man's father, wanting everything he had done to them to happen to him as well. She also cursed the townspeople.

Cathy, as a representative of her family line, began to pray through what the Lord had revealed. She first told the Lord her whole story of what had happened to her ancestors, sharing their hurts and responses. She then acknowledged the father's sins of being too concerned about what others think and not using his influence for good. She confessed the son's bitterness toward his father and the decisions he had made. She also acknowledged the woman's bitterness toward the father and the townspeople. Cathy confessed as sin the woman's negative decisions and the curses she made against the father and the people. In addition, Cathy forgave the townspeople and the father who had wounded the son and the woman and who had put all sorts of hurtful, public pronouncements upon them.

A few weeks later, Cathy shared some wonderful news. She had recently enjoyed something new with someone in leadership. This time, the leader wasn't only verbally supportive of her, but also he defended her in his actions, using his position of authority to bless her. In addition, she began to notice changes in her life in each of the themes that had been on her list. More importantly, the changes lasted. As a result, Cathy's skills and abilities continue to be welcomed almost everywhere she goes. She has continued to find favor and support with leadership, which has resulted in her being given many wonderful opportunities to minister to others.

Another thing changed about Cathy. I personally felt a noticeable change in her personage. Her presence, not just her words, now emanates a sense that she has something worthwhile to say, and that she is worth defending, endorsing, and supporting. She has become more at ease around authority figures. She no longer has to be on guard, compensating and being watchful for any negative reactions she had previously

13

learned to expect. All of these changes came about as a result of praying through some generational iniquities.

Often, before considering unresolved generational issues, it is important to consider any past unresolved experiences first. These are the events that took place during your life. Whether we realize it or not, certain events can significantly impact us. By addressing these first, it makes it easier to identify and address any possible generational issues.

In this chapter, I have provided a brief overview on how to identify past root causes that are the source to issues in the present. For a more in-depth understanding on this topic, I recommend my book: *Pray Through It*[1], which also provides many helpful insights, exercises and encouraging stories.

Bad Fruit from Bad Roots

How often have you experienced negative patterns in your life that keep recurring despite your efforts? If so, this is an indication that there are possible unresolved issues from your past that are manifesting in your present circumstances. These negative patterns are known as "bad fruit." The word "fruit" speaks of something being produced in your life, which can be positive or negative. This fruit is a natural byproduct of your choices, such as your actions, words and thoughts. Your choices are what determine what type of fruit, good or bad, will be produced in your life.

Galatians 6:7 says, "Do not be deceived, God is not mocked; for whatever a man sows, this he will also reap." This is the principle of sowing and reaping. "Sowing" happens whenever you make choices, as expressed through your actions, words or thoughts. Once sown, that choice is like a hidden seed that germinates. Eventually, it sprouts with the evidence of it manifesting in your life. The resulting fruit is the

---
[1] *Pray Through It* (ISBN: 978-0976354901) - available at Amazon.com.

"reaping," which contains characteristics of what was sown. If you sow apple seeds, you reap apple trees. If you sow weed seeds, you reap weeds.

So, whenever you see recurring bad fruit in your life, this is a strong indicator that you sowed bad seeds in your past. In such cases, and the fruit looks like the root cause. Keep in mind, not all negative things are because of past root causes, but it is definitely something to consider.

Whenever we sow a sinful response and give it enough time, it will produce bad fruit in our lives. One of the ways we sin is through our sinful responses to hurtful situations. Another person's behavior may have tempted us to react in a sinful manner. Our sinful response could be a number of things, such as resentment, or believing lies about ourselves, others, God, or life. And, like any seed buried beneath the soil, it is easy to forget about it. If left unchecked and given enough time, we'll eventually bear bad fruit.

Hebrews 12:15 says, "See to it that no one comes short of the grace of God; that no root of bitterness springing up causes trouble, and by it many be defiled." If we sow bitterness and don't repent, it will eventually affect our lives and others adversely. This is bad fruit.

Keep in mind that the reaping of bad fruit isn't dependent upon whether our feelings have changed since the past event. Nor is it dependent upon whether we have forgotten or chosen no longer to recall past events. Our choices sowed seeds. The reaping was set in motion. While our efforts to try harder, be different and do the right thing are beneficial, they won't overcome nor remove what was sown. Bad fruit will persist despite our efforts. Only one thing can remove the seeds sown and thus stop the reaping: prayers of confession and repentance to the Lord.

Bad fruit are those persistent negative responses and experiences that keep occurring despite your efforts. Have you found yourself asking any of the following questions (or ones like them)? This is a good indication of bad fruit in your life.

15

Here are some things to consider when consider something as bad fruit:

- Why do people seem to always reject me?
- Why do I seem to attract men (or women) who are _____?
- Why don't my circumstances change, no matter what I do?
- Just fill in the blank: Why does _____ keep happening?

Keep in mind that while you seek the Lord for healing, He expects you to persevere and continue to be obedient and do the right things, despite that you struggle with the bad fruit. In the meantime, God will use this process to develop character in your life. One thing is for sure. These recurring negative issues provide clues about what in your past needs to be addressed and healed.

The following are key characteristics of bad fruit, which strongly indicate that the root cause is from unresolved issues in your past.

Key Characteristics of Bad Fruit

Fruitful (Matthew 7:16) – Is there a repeated manifestation of bad fruit in your life? Is so, what is it?

Persistent (Jeremiah 12:13) – Does the bad fruit persist despite your efforts to prune it?

Seasonal (Galatians 6:9) – Does the bad fruit have seasons, recurring at certain times or in certain situations or with certain people?

Increasing (Matthew 13:23b) – In some areas, have you seen an increase of the bad fruit?

As with any issue, the first step is to recognize something as bad fruit. Once you do this, the characteristics of the bad fruit will provide insight into what the root cause will look like. The two will be similar. For instance, if you have recurring trust issues, chances are you have unresolved trust issues in your past. The seeds sown in your past are your sinful responses and the lies you believed. Once identified, you then commit these, in prayer of confession and repentance, to the Lord Jesus. This is how the root causes are removed.

The following is how to pray to the Lord through root causes. The first part involves your mind: tell your story. The second part involves your heart: share your feelings. And the last part involves your will: make a choice to confess, forgive and renounce despite how you may or may not feel. If possible, do this with someone else. This allows another person to pray with you while pronouncing forgiveness over you. In addition, the other person can pray for any healing as needed and can pray a blessing over you as well.

Praying through Root Issues
- Tell the Lord your story about the past hurtful event.
- Share with the Lord how you felt when it happened.
- Confess to the Lord your sinful responses.
- Forgive those who hurt and offended you.
- Renounce any negative decisions you had made or lies you had believed.

Identifying Possible Generational Iniquities
Before concluding that a repetitive, negative experience (the bad fruit) has been caused by unresolved generational issues, it is highly recommended that you consider your own past experiences first. Identifying and praying through roots in your own past often resolves the ongoing bad fruit. If anything persists after this, it may be an indicator of unresolved generational issues.

When considering if the bad fruit is connected to an unresolved generational issue, first explore known family history, including family accounts and written records. In some instances, you may already know of family stories you have never thought were connected to generational iniquities until now. Check out whether the stories have a similar theme as the

17

bad fruit you have identified. If so, this is what you need to commit to prayer, confessing the iniquities committed.

Next, ask the Lord that if there are any generational iniquities related to the bad fruit, that He would reveal any family history you are unaware of. Be sure to ask open-ended questions like, "Is there something related to this issue that is generational?" No assumption is being made. Avoid close-ended questions like, "Where in the past generations did something similar happen?" Such questions are based on the assumption that something in the past did happen. In other words, do not ask questions that communicate that you are looking for a predetermined answer.

Whatever is retrieved through prayer, hold it loosely. Don't consider what you hear to be absolute fact. Instead, pray about what you think was revealed, knowing that if it is true, the fruit of your prayer will confirm or disconfirm it.

If the Lord does not reveal to you anything, that's alright. Perhaps there is no generational iniquity connected to what you are considering as bad fruit. Or, it is not time for the Lord to show you yet. So it is good idea just to ask the Lord that if there is a generational iniquity and when it is time that He would reveal it.

 Things to Consider

- What are some of the bad fruit in your life? Make a list of some specific examples.
- What characteristics seem to indicate that these incidents are bad fruit?
- What specific memories and events come to mind that could indicate root causes? What were your sinful reactions? Make a list.
- Referring to the list of steps on the previous page, pray through the root causes with help from a friend.

Sin, Transgression and Iniquity

The LORD, the LORD God, compassionate and gracious,
slow to anger, and abounding in lovingkindness and truth;
who keeps lovingkindness for thousands,
who forgives iniquity, transgression and sin…
Exodus 34:6b-7a

Selective Hearing

eresa was a missionary who had recently returned to the United States. While on the mission field, she became familiar with the spiritual warfare that often occurs when dealing with those who are resisting the gospel. At times, her very life was threatened because of a witchdoctor who didn't want the people to turn to Jesus. The witchdoctor didn't want to lose his control over the people. Fortunately, Teresa could hear God's voice, and He would tell her what to do in the midst of the spiritual warfare. Although she experienced many difficulties, she did have many wonderful things happen.

But despite these things, and her knowing that God is good, Teresa felt hurt by God. Her knowledge of Him wasn't enough to overcome the hurt she felt in her heart. Though the Lord told her what to do in the midst of warfare, it seemed to her that He never warned her prior to the attacks. Such forewarnings would have helped her to be prepared. She now suffered from ongoing back pain that felt as if someone had stabbed her with a spear. She felt that this could have been prevented if God had warned her in advance. In addition, her back pain affected her ability to sleep. As a result, she was beginning to distrust God. She feared that He would ask her to do something but then let her be attacked without warning.

We asked the Lord to give us insight. The Lord revealed that, though Teresa could hear Him well, something was

19

preventing her from hearing His warnings. It was as if she had selective hearing, hearing only God's directives but not His warnings. But why?

As we began to explore Teresa's life, she shared how her parents had attended and then joined a religious cult. She had tried to warn her parents that this wasn't right, that it taught erroneous doctrine and teachings, but they wouldn't listen. The Lord also revealed that others in her family line had done the same thing. They too had turned a deaf ear to those the Lord sent to warn them not to get involved.

In prayer, Teresa shared the ways in which her parents didn't listen to her warnings. She then forgave them while confessing her judgments against them. In addition, she confessed the iniquities of her ancestors: getting involved in religious cult, not listening to those whom God had sent to warn them, and turning a deaf ear to God.

After she prayed, Teresa mentioned something she hadn't shared before. All of the women in her family have had a 30% physical hearing loss, including Teresa. So, I prayed a short prayer that the Lord would heal her hearing loss as well.

The next day, Teresa shared some wonderful news. For one, she had actually slept through the night for the first time in a long time. The pain in her back was gone. But there was more! Each day when Teresa came for ministry, she had passed by some flagpoles outside of the building. But something was different that day. For the first time in her life, she could hear the sound of a flag waving in the breeze. Her physical hearing had been healed as well!

In the Scriptures, the Hebrew language often uses different words when referring to the wrongs committed against God and others. The most common words are: *chatta' ah*[2], *avon*[3]

---

[2] *chatta' ah* (חטאה) is pronounced chattâ'âh (khat-taw-aw'), [H2403] Strong's Exhaustive Concordance, 1890

and *pesha*[4]. These words are often translated as "sin," "iniquity," and "transgression" (or "trespass"). At first glance, one might assume that these words are synonyms. If this were true, it would be reasonable to assume that they could be used interchangeably.

While this might be true in for these English words, it isn't so for their Hebrew counterparts. If you were to study the Hebrew, you would find that, while there are similarities between these words, there are distinct differences as well. And, if you study the Bible with these differences in mind, you'll begin to understand that God had a very good reason to use each word distinctly in specific instances. With this in mind, let's look at the Hebrew meaning of these words, starting with "sin," then "transgression," and lastly, "iniquity."

Sin

The Hebrew word *chatta' ah* is derived from the word *chata*,[5] and are both translated as "sin." The word *chata* means "to miss," as in, "to miss the mark" or target. God sets a standard of how we are to live, and whenever we fail to meet that standard, we have sinned. Therefore, "sin" is anytime we fall short of God's standard – whether we know better or not.

God created us with fantastic qualities – with talents, dreams, abilities, purpose, curiosity, creativity, destiny, and more. He also intended us for relationship with Him and to participate in His glory. He designed us with this in mind - that life would go best as you operate by His design, in sync with His plan. This involves staying in relationship with Him and living in a manner that demonstrates the truth about ourselves, others, God, and life as He designed it.

So, sin is whenever we have diverted from His plan, believing lies about ourselves, others, God and life. This is especially evident whenever we act on those lies through our actions, words and thoughts.

---

[3] *avon* (עוֹן) is pronounced ʿâvôn (aw-vone), [H5771], ibid Strong's
[4] *pesha*ʿ (פשע) is pronounced pehʾ·shah, [H6588], ibid Strong's
[5] *chata* (חטא) is pronounced châṭâ' (khaw-taw'), [H2401], ibid Strong's

21

Transgression

The Hebrew word *pesha* is derived from the word *pasha*[6], and both are commonly translated as "transgression," meaning "to break away" or "revolt." It is also sometimes translated as "trespass" or "rebellion."

These Hebrew words (*pesha* and *pasha*) are often used when referring to the rebellious manner in which someone sins. In other words, they're more specific to rebellion than to just "missing the mark."

For example, Job 31:33 says, "Have I covered my transgressions like Adam, by hiding my iniquity in my bosom..." Another instance occurred when Israel committed transgressions by rebelling against the house of David after his death (II Chronicles 10:19). They had rebelled by refusing to submit to the authority of David's household.

Iniquity

The Hebrew word for iniquity is *avon*. Its literal meaning is "perversity," i.e. moral evil. It is an evil inclination, a motivation, but not an obligation, to behave and think in a sinful way. Its root meaning is "to bend" or "make crooked." It happens whenever something God created is altered or changed from its intended design and purpose.

For instance, God designed communication. Within His wonderful design, He intended for us not to lie to one another, but to be truthful. He intended it this way for our benefit, that life would go better if we communicated without lying.

Trust is broken when we lie. So when we decide that it's okay to lie in some instances (what some call "white lies"), we are altering or bending God's design. Though it might seem harmless, we're making crooked, even so slightly, God's definition of what telling the truth is. In so doing, we are perverting God's design, watering it down and lowering His standard. When we allow such alterations to become acceptable, we begin to make a sin into an iniquity.

---

[6] *pasha`* (פשע) is pronounced paw·shah', [H6586], ibid Strong's

22

An iniquity is whenever we make a particular sin acceptable, rationalizing it away. It is when we make it a way of life and a way of thinking. It's when a sin becomes what we would call a sinful habit or practice. In such a case, a sin has become a stronghold, having been given power over us through our tolerance and yielding to temptation. Thus, it gains the means to influence us and even our circumstances.

An iniquity is when we settle for less than God's best design. It is when we alter the truth about God, ourselves, others, and life. It is when we begin to redefine things other than how God defines them, and we begin to embrace and live by these altered definitions as if they are truth. Left unconfronted and unrepented of, these become an influence in our lives, tempting us to think, respond, and act in ways that are in keeping with our iniquity. Though they don't have the power to control us, they now become one more factor influencing us to respond in sinful ways. In most cases, they eventually become unchallenged, as if they were normal aspects of our lives.

Ignorance of God and His ways doesn't make one immune. Many people commit iniquities and are under their influence but don't even know it. Some do know it, but have grown accustomed to it and either don't care or don't know what to do.

The most obvious example of an iniquity is when someone attempts to get better at a particular sin. An example would be a thief who considers how he can improve his robbing skills, or an adulterer who thinks about ways to be more seductive. Scripture refers to people like this as "those who work iniquity" or "a worker of iniquity" (Job 31:3, Psalms 141:4, Proverbs 10:29). In these instances, the word "iniquity" is the Hebrew word *aven*.[7] Workers of iniquity are people who are trying to get better at sinning, or are attempting to improve their skills for sinful purposes.

In some cases, one didn't consciously purpose to get better at sinning, but ended up doing so through ongoing sin. An example would be repetitive sexual sin or giving in to rages or

---

[7] *aven* (און) is pronounced 'âven (*aw'-ven*), [H205], ibid Strong's

23

addictions. What one thought one could control now has control over him or her. Thus, it has become a sinful habit. An addiction is an example of this. By forming an addiction, one has created one's own sinful inclination or disposition through practice and by not resisting. This is why David said (Psalms 32:5):

I acknowledged my sin [*chatta' ah*] to You and my iniquity [*avon*] I did not hide. I said, "I will confess my transgressions [*pesha*] to the LORD"; And You forgave the guilt [*avon*] of my sin [*chatta' ah*].

In saying this, David is acknowledging his responsibility for his iniquity that resulted from his sin.

Often, when we think of iniquity, we think of obvious evil intentions and blatant wicked deeds. Though this is true, iniquity can also be more subtle than this. It's the more subtle iniquities that people tend to overlook. And sadly, they have agreed to tolerate these as well. For iniquity isn't based upon the intensity of the wrongdoing, but rather upon what sin one has allowed to become a way of life or thinking. It makes no difference whether one is aware of it or not. It is still an iniquity.

Sometimes in scripture, *avon* can refer to the consequences often associated with committing sin, like David's guilt expressed in Psalm 32. The context is what indicates which aspect of iniquity is being emphasized.

Categories of Iniquities

Iniquities tend to fall into one of three categories: personal, communal, and generational. It is the context of the passage that clarifies which category of iniquity is being addressed.

Personal Iniquities

Personal iniquities are those that an individual has committed (I Chronicles 21:8). They are any sinful ways of thinking and/or acting that a person has allowed to become a habit or way of life. These might be minor sinful behaviors

24

which one has justified, minimized or surrendered to, by saying to oneself, "This is just the way I am." In so doing, one has redefined what is considered acceptable behavior, thus excusing one's iniquity. But God doesn't make sinful personality traits. We all have aspects of ourselves with which we struggle and may dislike, but we still can choose how to deal with them.

The Bible speaks more about personal iniquities than any other type. This means that it's very important that we each deal with our own iniquities. The longer we fail to deal with them, the more accustomed we become to them. Not only do we risk allowing them to increase their influence in our own lives (Psalms 38:4), but also we risk them being passed on to our descendants (Exodus 20:5). But as long as we are wrestling against and confessing our sins, we prevent those sins from becoming iniquities.

Communal Iniquities

Communal iniquities are the second type of iniquities. These are ones committed by a group of people or community. Examples would include, but are not limited to: cities, people groups, nations, organizations, businesses, corporations and governments.

Some examples of communal iniquities would be: caste or class systems, genocide, racism and oppression of women. They can also include illegal practices committed by an organization, such as tax evasion, injustices, taking bribes and embezzlements.

An example of a communal iniquity in the Bible occurred when the Israelites refused to enter the Promised Land. They chose to obey their fears, despite all the miracles God had shown them (Numbers 13—14). Ten times, they acted in a similar manner, thus illustrating that their sinful response had become their way of life.

25

Generational Iniquities

The third category of iniquity is generational, which is the primary focus of this book. Generational iniquities are those we have inherited from our ancestors and which we pass on to our descendants. Often, without even realizing it, these have a tremendous impact on our lives, as well as on the lives of others. In the next chapter, we will begin to look at the significance of generational iniquities.

Note, while reading this book, unless otherwise stated, every time the word "iniquity" is used, it refers to the Hebrew word *avon*. Whenever the word "sin" is used, it refers to the Hebrew word *chatta' ah*. And whenever the word "transgression" is used, it refers to the Hebrew word *pesha*. This is for consistency and to avoid any confusion.

 Things to Consider

- What are some new insights you have gained here about the differences between sin, transgression, and iniquity (as the Hebrew defines them)?
- What is an example of how a sin becomes a personal iniquity? How do you think this happens?
- What are some examples of communal iniquities you have seen, such as in a community, city or nation?

Generational Iniquity

We have sinned, committed iniquity,
acted wickedly and rebelled,
even turning aside from
Your commandments and ordinances.
Moreover, we have not listened to
Your servants the prophets,
who spoke in Your name to our kings, our princes,
our fathers and all the people of the land.
Daniel 9:5-6

Fear of Mushrooms

few years ago, Anne began to grow concerned for her son, Matt. He had developed some strange and unfounded fears – fears that started out as minor, but grew into something much bigger. Despite all her efforts to help her son, he seemed to be getting worse, and she was becoming weary. His issue consumed so much time and energy, and her efforts only brought temporary relief for Matt. And sometimes, no matter what she did, it didn't make any difference at all.

Matt feared that if he touched something that was considered dirty or poisonous, he would get sick and die. Though Matt knew this wasn't true, the fear still felt very real to him. Despite all of the consoling and prayer he received and his efforts to resist, his feelings would neither change nor go away. His fears of getting ill or dying were persistent, constantly occupying his thoughts despite all of the consoling and even prayer he had received. For some reason, mushrooms and pencils had become a particular concern for him. Even though he knew that pencils aren't made of the element lead, he still feared getting lead poisoning. He felt compelled to wash his hands whenever he came into contact with one of these items (or even a person or object that had!). As a result, he washed his hands so often that they were constantly chapped.

Another thing that became evident was that Matt was extremely aware of the feelings of others. In fact, we soon discovered that as a little boy, he often felt his father's insecurities. Because of this sensitivity and his love for his father, he made a decision in his heart of: "I will take the burden," thinking he could somehow help.

So, we asked the Lord what was the source of the insecurities of Matt's father. He revealed that Matt's father had fears he was unwilling to face. It wasn't wrong that he was afraid. Rather, it was that he gave into his fears instead of being willing to learn to conquer them. The Lord wouldn't have asked him to face something he couldn't eventually overcome. Unfortunately, Matt's father had chosen to run from his fears, leaving behind a deposit of unresolved feelings of fear. And Matt, without knowing better or knowing the history of his father's denial, took these fears upon himself, thinking that they were his own fears.

Concerning Matt's father, the Lord showed us some details about his fears. The Lord had brought opportunities for Matt's father to face his fears. Whenever this happened, he became afraid, which was to be expected. But instead of asking the Lord for help, he focused on his sense of inadequacy and acted upon that.

The Lord revealed to Matt that Matt's paternal grandfather had acted similarly. Grandpa turned to alcohol to drown his fears instead of facing them. So, Matt's father had been influenced by his own father's unresolved fears. And now, Matt was being influenced by the iniquities of both men.

In an attempt to avoid their fears, Matt's father and grandfather had believed lies and made similar decisions. Decisions like: "God asks too much of me;" "It is too scary to do what God asks of me;" "I can never do what God is asking me to do;" "It is more than I can handle;" and, "I am bound to fail."

With this information, I led Matt to confess in prayer the iniquities of his father and grandfather. He acknowledged how, when God approached them, they both gave in to their fears instead of facing them. He included how they decided not to do what God had asked, but instead chose to live their own lives. Most of all, Matt renounced the various decisions they had made to not face their fears in response to the lies they had believed. Matt also surrendered his decision to "take the burden."

I saw Matt two weeks later. He had good news. He was no longer struggling with his fear of mushrooms and pencils. He was no longer overly concerned with germs or with washing his hands. He was more confident. When the old feelings did come back, he told himself that they weren't his to carry, and they left. He now reminds himself that though he senses others' feelings, it isn't his job to take those feelings upon himself. He knows now that God allows him to sense such things so he can help by praying for others and offering advice. But in the end, it is the other person's responsibility to face their own issues.

Previously to this time of ministry, Matt was being influenced by the iniquities of his father and grandfather, which manifested in Matt's irrational fears. His misplaced fear of mushrooms and pencils was really an attempt to objectify or make sense of what he felt from others. This is is why any methods to find relief were only temporal, since the real source hadn't been addressed. But once the source was identified and prayed through, Matt found real, lasting relief.

As stated earlier, generational iniquities are those our ancestors have committed. They're also those that we have committed, which get passed on to our descendants. Generational iniquities produce negative tendencies in family lines that influence subsequent generations to behave in manners similar as one's ancestors. Often, these inherited influences go unquestioned and are considered "normal." Some might even say, "This is just the way we are as a family," and not even question it. In some ways, sin (*chatta' ah*) and iniquity (*avon*) are similar. They both negatively affect our relationship with God and others (Isaiah 51:2), and they both require confession for their removal. However, in the Old Testament, the manner by which sin was to be addressed was quite different than dealing with iniquity.

> The Torah speaks of a 'sin offering' but never an offering to remove iniquity. The Torah speaks of 'bearing iniquity' but never 'bearing sin.' They are clearly quite different concepts, even though our modern English has improperly slurred them together. Orthodox Judaism understands iniquity, calling it 'the evil inclination.' For the most part, Conservative and Reform Judaism have lost sight of this important concept.[8]

For the ceremony of the Day of Atonement (Leviticus 16), the priests were required to choose two goats. They would sacrifice the first goat as a sin offering to the Lord. The second goat was known as the "scapegoat" and was to be offered for atonement. Concerning the scapegoat (Leviticus 16:21), the high priest was to:

> ...lay both his hands on the head of the live goat, confess over it all the iniquities of the children of Israel, and all their transgressions, concerning all their sins, putting them on the head of the goat, and shall send it away into the wilderness by the hand of a suitable man. The goat shall bear on itself all their iniquities...

---

[8] *Introduction to Messianic Judaism, chatta'* (sin) & *'avon* (iniquity), Shema Yisrael, Rabbi Jim Appel, 2007

As I will share in more detail in a later chapter, Jesus became our scapegoat. He was the atonement for our sins, and He bore our iniquities.

Misunderstandings about Iniquity Versus Sin

Not knowing the difference between the meanings of the Hebrew words *chatta' ah* and *avon* have unfortunately led to several misunderstandings. As a result, this has hindered us from gaining greater insights and applications from Scripture.

One misunderstanding is: we inherit our ancestors' sins. While we do inherit inclinations toward sin through our ancestors, Scripture makes it very clear that we don't inherit our ancestors' sins (*chatta' ah*). However, we do inherit their iniquities (*avon*). The phrase, "visiting the iniquity of the fathers" (which some Bibles have translated *avon* in some instances as "sin" instead of "iniquity") is used in many places in Scripture. However, in every instance or variation of this phrase, the word *avon* is used exclusively; never the word *chatta' ah*. Therefore, this distinction between "sin" and "iniquity" must be extremely important. Later, we will explore just how important it is.

Another misunderstanding is that we may believe we are bound to commit the same sins and iniquities as our forefathers. While generational iniquity has the power to influence, it doesn't have the power to control us. We have free will. And with our free will, we make choices either to submit to influences or to resist them. Therefore, we aren't destined to be just like our forefathers in their sinful ways, though we may struggle with similar issues.

When we take a look at the lives of some of the ancestors in Jesus' genealogy, we see this very principle (see Matthew 1:7-8). The following are some of the fathers and sons in His family line:

Rehoboam begat Abijah: a bad father had a bad son.
Abijah begat Asa: a bad father had a good son.
Asa begat Jehoshaphat: a good father had good son.
Jehoshaphat begat Joram: a good father had bad son.

31

A bad father doesn't guarantee producing a bad son, nor does a good father guarantee having a good son. Doing good or bad is a choice, no matter what our lineage may be like. There is no excuse for bad behavior, regardless of our family line. The Bible clearly states that, "Each of us will give an account of himself to God" (Romans 14:12). You won't be giving an account for your father's choices, nor for any of your ancestors'. But you will for your own words, thoughts, and deeds.

What you do inherit from your ancestors is the influence from what they did. The choice is yours, either to walk in the same manner or not. It is up to you to resist the influence of the generational iniquity and sow good character and blessings into your family line.

So, how did the words "sin" and "iniquity" come to be seen as interchangeable?

One reason is that many of us have been improperly taught so we didn't know any difference. Many teachers continue to use these words interchangeably, simply because they don't know better. And we don't second guess this because it is engrained in our way of thinking.

Another reason is that, in some translations of the Bible[9], the Hebrew word *avon* is translated as "iniquity" in one passage and "sin" in another. And the same goes for the word *chatta' ah*. This has resulted in readers thinking that there is no difference between the two words.

For example, in some translations, one passage reads, "the sins of the father," while the same phrase in the same translation in a different part of the Bible reads, "the iniquities of the fathers." However, the Hebrew word *avon* is used in both passages. This causes us as the reader to think that the words are interchangeable, and thus, we miss important truths in what the Lord is saying.

---

[9] The King James Version translation of the Bible consistently translated the Hebrew word *avon* as "iniquity" when referring to "the iniquity of the fathers."

Also, when we read the Bible, it is easy to assume that certain passages were written in certain ways for poetic emphasis: that, rather than sounding redundant by using the same words over and over again, the writer used different words with similar meanings in order to say the same thing. Since this style is often used in poetry and other writings, it is easy to assume that this is what is being done in Scriptures. However, this isn't the case. As we study the Scriptures, we begin to understand that there are reasons why different Hebrew words are used, especially in the same text.

The following are some other examples of when both *avon* and *chatta' ah* were used in the same verse:

Psalms 51:2: "Wash me thoroughly from my iniquity [*avon*] and cleanse me from my sin [*chatta' ah*]. For I know my transgressions [*pesha*], and my sin [*chatta' ah*] is ever before me."

Proverbs 5:22: "His own iniquities [*avon*] will capture the wicked. And he will be held with the cords of his sin [*chatta' ah*]."

Isaiah 59:2: "But your iniquities [*avon*] have made a separation between you and your God. And your sins [*chatta' ah*] have hidden His face from you so that He doesn't hear."

When we read passages like these, it can be easy to think that they were written this way to emphasize the importance of what was being stated. In other words, if something is repeated through the use of what appears to be synonyms, it must be important. While this is often true, it isn't always the case. And when we make that assumption, we tend to look no further and end up missing deeper insights.

So how did this misunderstanding between *avon* and *chatta' ah* happen in the first place?

33

Who or what started this linguistic confusion? The blurring of sin and iniquity began with the Greek language. The Greek language has only one word, *hamartia*, to mean both sin and iniquity. *Hamartia* is always translated "sin" in the New Testament, even though its context shows it can mean either sin or iniquity.[10]

The meaning of the Greek word *hamartia*[11] is broader, in that it encompasses the meaning of both *chatta' ah* and *avon*. So, the meaning of *hamartia* depends upon two things: its usage in the passage, and viewing it in the context of the Hebrew understanding of sin and iniquity.

For instance, Romans 4:7-8 is a quote of Psalms 32:1-2. Psalms 32:1-2 contains all three Hebrew words of *pesha* (transgression), *chatta' ah* (sin) and *avon* (iniquity), in that order. However, in Romans 4:7-8, *chatta' ah* and *avon* were both translated into the Greek word, *hamartia*. Hebrews 8:12 is another example, as it is a reference to Jeremiah 31:34.

Another example is when Jesus' disciples asked Him why a particular man was blind (John 9:1-3). The question they asked indicates they understood the principle that the parents' iniquities do influence one's descendants: "Rabbi, who sinned, this man or his parents, that he would be born blind?" When we read this in the context of the Hebrew understanding of "sin" and "iniquity," what they were asking was: "Was it because of the man's own sin or the iniquity of his parents that he was born blind?" While, in this case, Jesus made it clear that the man wasn't blind for either reason, He didn't dismiss the truth that negative influences from generational iniquities do occur.

Later, in the same passage (v. 34), the Pharisees also demonstrated that they were aware of the Hebrew understanding of "sin" versus "iniquity," since they accused the man of being "born entirely in sins" (*hamartia*), referring to

---

[10] Ibid: *Introduction to Messianic Judaism*

[11] *hamartia* (ἁμαρτία) is pronounced *ham-ar-tee'-ah*, [G266] ibid, Strong's

34

his parents. This indicates that they assumed (though incorrectly, in this instance) that the man had been blind because of generational iniquity, that being of his parents'.

This shows how important it is that we don't immediately conclude that, when something bad has happened, it is because of generational iniquity. We need to consider it, perhaps, but not assume. One thing the Pharisees did do right, at least this time, was to inquire of the Lord (i.e., "Rabbi, who sinned, this man or his parents, that he would be born blind?"). And so should we.

Another New Testament passage to consider is Matthew 23, when Jesus confronted the Pharisees. He told them that they are no different than their forefathers, who murdered the prophets. Acts 7:51 is a similar Scripture. These passages illustrate how the iniquities of the forefathers had indeed influenced their descendants.

This all said, we now see how much richer the Scriptures become when we read them with an understanding of the original language and context. When we read the New Testament, we need to take into consideration the truths taught in the Old Testament.

Things to Consider

- Go back a few pages and reread each of the verses listed that contain both the words "sin" and "iniquity." What are some deeper insights that can be found now, knowing the full meanings of the words?
- In what ways have you seen people in your family line fall to the influence of generational iniquities?
- In what ways have you seen people attempt to resist negative patterns in their family line? How successful has that been?
- What are some misunderstandings you have had about sin and iniquity? Where do you think you learned this way of thinking?

We and Our Fathers

...for we have sinned against the LORD our God,
we and our fathers,
from our youth even to this day.
And we have not obeyed the voice of the LORD our God.
Jeremiah 3:25

No Matter How Hard You Try

or years, William struggled, unable to get ahead in his career or his finances. No matter how hard he tried, nothing seemed to make a difference. Having been disappointed so many times, he had given up expecting change and had become pessimistic. So, when he and his wife came for help, it was only because she wanted to. He didn't see any point in him coming too.

In the midst of this inability to get ahead, William felt that God was to blame. Throughout his life, he had sought to be obedient to the Lord in whatever he did, trying to seek and honor God in everything. Yet, despite William's loyalty, God seemed to take away the good things in his life. While William tried to be thankful for what he did have, his thankfulness was superficial and short-lived. For it seemed that, eventually, something always happened that brought back all of the old frustrations and feelings of futility.

This experience had become such a part of William's life that he finally resigned himself to the belief that this is just the way life is and that there is nothing he can do about it. He began to question why he put so much energy into a relationship with God when it wouldn't make any difference. Being stuck made him feel powerless, which made him angry and depressed. So he decided not to expect change and not to expect God to come through.

36

Most of his life, William had done work he enjoyed. But during the last several years, he had a job that was unfulfilling and paid very little. This fueled his frustration. He began to feel that he was doomed to live out the rest of his life doing something he hated while struggling to make ends meet. What made things even more frustrating was his recent experiences of being rejected every time he applied for a different job. This added to his sense of futility, especially at his age. He was becoming more pessimistic, expecting to be disappointed. As a result, he felt there was nothing to look forward to in his future.

In addition, William's and his wife's financial situation was extremely troubling to him. He couldn't stand watching the money they had saved over the years disappear. Here he had worked and worked all of his life, and now, in his fifties, there was little to nothing to show for it.

Despite William's wife receiving an inheritance, this seemed to make no difference, as various expenses quickly absorbed it. William foresaw that it would soon be gone and, once again, there would be nothing left for their future.

Looking back over William's life, there appeared to be various events that contributed to his worldview. At age five, William's father had died in a plane crash, and William was left with a mother he couldn't stand. As a boy, he felt powerless. His mother was controlling, and he didn't have a father to protect him. It was at this point that William decided he wanted nothing to do with God, since God had allowed his father to die and had left him with a controlling mother. But as life went on, William forgot that he had made this decision. As a result, he had no idea this was the reason his heart kept God at arm's length. This was despite his attempts as an adult to seek a relationship with Him.

William's mother eventually remarried. But, when his stepfather died, it reopened the wound he had gotten from his biological father. So, in his heart, he decided, "There will be no one there for me," and, "It's all up to me."

William also recalled a time, as a boy, when he mowed the lawn, which was huge. He did this without being told, in an attempt to do something special for his parents. But despite his efforts, he received no praise.

So, we made a list of various childhood issues, and William prayed through them. Afterwards, his inner turmoil and anger began to subside. However, the feeling of, "No matter how hard you try, it won't make any difference" didn't go away.

As we took a closer look at William's family, we discovered this same theme. It was something that all of the men in his family had struggled with as well. It was almost like an unspoken family motto.

One such time was when William's stepfather had lost his business. After five years of effort, he had built it into something successful. But, in one day, he lost it only because he had lost his lease. The landlord was unwilling to renew it. As a result, his business became worthless. He couldn't even sell it. He declared bankruptcy and lost his house as well. He had to start all over again. Eventually, he got a job but was laid off. These setbacks had tempted William's stepfather to become resentful. Two weeks later, he died of a heart attack.

So, in prayer, William shared with God about his stepfather's tragic loss and how he had become resentful, deciding that "No matter how hard I try, it won't make any difference." He also confessed that his grandfather had made a similar decision. Lastly, he confessed this generational decision as sin and renounced it.

What was interesting was that, during our sessions together, William didn't feel any emotional connection to any of the things he prayed. Even afterwards, he didn't feel any different. But the important thing was that he had been willing to pray through the things the Lord had revealed, leaving the results to God.

Prior to our last session, William once again applied for another job. Based upon past experience, he had no hope of getting the position, but one has to give him credit for not giving up despite how he felt. About six weeks later, an amazing thing happened. William received a call saying that he and his wife had been accepted as caretakers for a large estate. The owners lived at the estate only part of the year, so they

38

needed someone to be there year round to take care of the land and the house. William and his wife were given a salary, free room and board, and their own separate house on the property. Now, they could live and make use of a place that was beyond their ability to ever afford and yet not have the responsibility of owning it. Not only this, but also the estate was located in one of William's favorite places – Montana – where he loves to hike, fish and hunt. God certainly made a difference for William, blessing him in ways he had never imagined.

Fathers

In the Hebrew, *ab*[12] is the word for "father." Depending on the context, it can also refer to one's forefathers. This would be one's father, grandfathers, great grandfathers, and so on – all of the men from whom one has descended.

So, when the Bible says that the iniquities of the fathers pass to subsequent generations, "fathers" includes forefathers as well. But what about the generational influence of the mothers? And is it possible to inherit generational influence through one's stepparents by adoption or remarriage?

In the New Testament, Jesus' genealogy is listed in two places: Matthew 1:1-17 and Luke 3:23-37. The genealogy in Matthew is of Joseph's family line, and the one in Luke is of Mary's family line. Joseph's family line is traced back to Abraham, while Mary's is traced back to Adam. One of the amazing things that stand out is that the prophetic promise given to David was fulfilled through both lineages[13] (Jeremiah 23:5).

Joseph isn't Jesus' biological father. God the Father is, via the Holy Spirit. Joseph is Jesus' stepfather. In addition, Joseph is Jesus' adoptive father, making Jesus grafted into Joseph's

---

[12] *ab* (אב) is pronounced âb (awb), [H1], ibid, Strong's
[13] Joseph is the descendant of David via David's son Solomon, and Mary is via David's son Nathan.

family line. Therefore, by Joseph's obedience to God, Jesus was entitled to all that comes to an actual biological son. If it weren't possible to inherit through one's stepfather and/or adoptive father, Jesus would have no inheritance through Joseph. And, therefore, there would be no need to list Joseph's genealogy.

Mary is Jesus' biological mother, which makes them genetically related. If generational inheritance didn't pass through mothers, then there would be no need to list Mary's lineage. Yet, the significance of this is that Jesus is a descendant of David, fulfilling God's promise to David through her family line.

As a result, Jesus is a direct descendant of King David both by adoption and blood. Through Joseph, Jesus obtained the legal right to His lineage; through Mary, he inherited His humanity; and, through God the Father, Jesus has His divinity. This is why he was called the Son of Man as well as the Son of God. Both Joseph's and Mary's lineages establish the fact that generational influences do come through stepparents (which includes adoption) as well as through one's mother.

In John 9:1-3, it is clear that it was known that a generational influence could come through one's mother. The reference is to the blind man's "parents" (father and mother), not just the father.

The story "Always Left Behind" in the chapter titled "Visiting the Generations" is an example of a generational iniquity that came through the mother's side of the family. The same is true for the story titled "Utter Destruction" in the back of this book. In both instances, when a descendant confessed the generational iniquity, something significant in his or her life changed.

When we become Christians, we are adopted by God the Father (Romans 8:14-23). Thus, we are all called "children of God" and "sons of God."[14] And, by adoption into God's family, we have an inheritance from our heavenly Father (Galatians

---

[14] For more passages on this subject, see Matthew 5:9; John 1:12; Romans 9:4; Galatians 3:26; Ephesians 1:5; Philippians 2:15; I John 3:1-2; 4:4.

40

4:5-7, Ephesians 1:14-18, I Peter 1:4). This isn't unlike when someone is adopted or has stepparents. In such a case, that person comes underneath another person's parental authority and dominion. So, whatever good or bad things that parent does, the one adopted becomes a recipient. This includes iniquities.

Biological ancestors seem to have much more significant impact than step or adoptive ancestors. This is most likely due to being biologically related. Even so, it is definitely worth investigating the history of one's step-ancestors and ancestors by adoption when considering the source of a generational iniquity. The significance of this was seen in the story at the beginning of this chapter.

Things to Consider

- How has this chapter changed your perspective about how you view your ancestors?
- If you have any ancestors who were stepparents or parents by adoption, what influences do you think you may have inherited?
- What applications and conclusions can you make, knowing that Jesus had individuals in His family line who weren't good?

Generational Visitation

Our fathers sinned, and are no more;
It is we who have borne their iniquities.
Lamentations 5:7

Animosity between Father and Son

When my son, Tim, was about eight, a new dynamic began to develop in our relationship. He and I would often get into discussions about various topics. At first, I thought this was good, since I never got to dialogue with my own father. But, as time passed, the discussions turned into debates, and we found ourselves becoming more argumentative. It was no longer enjoyable. I had to fight to keep from getting angry. To make things worse, there never seemed to be any resolution.

This dynamic occurred whenever we got into a disagreement. During such times, we would suddenly become very stubborn, and we found ourselves being tempted not to consider the other's point of view, demanding our own perspective. It was as though a strong, invisible force was pushing us neither to admit fault nor to reconcile with each other.

Whenever this happened, I struggled with wanting not to forgive my son and wanting to be mean and punitive. It got to the point where it took just about everything I had to keep my temper from getting out of control. Sometimes I felt justified. I would say to myself, "I am the father, and my son is the child. He needs to respect me!" Despite that my son's actions at the time may have been inappropriate, I still had my part to play, resisting the temptation to overreact and needing to own up to the times if I did.

There were times I had to walk away in order to prevent things from escalating. It was as if something compelled us to

42

become overly argumentative, making it difficult to think rationally.

In addition to this, I often had to spend time cleaning up after the arguments – or, should I say, "battles." This often involved me apologizing for yelling, overreacting, etc. There were times I didn't even want to reconcile with my son, but I would do it anyway, even though it was difficult. It was an ongoing cycle. But this was all I knew to do, since the Lord hadn't given me any insight even though I had been asking Him in prayer. I thought, "Why does this keep happening, despite all my efforts?" Tim and I were getting tired of all of this. This struggle went on for two years.

One day, when Tim and I were in the midst of another argument, the Lord gave me an insight. He said, "There is generational animosity between father and son. And it is on both sides." The Lord was indicating that Tim was getting a double dose of generational influence, since it was coming from my wife's side of the family as well as my own.

Later, I looked up the meaning of the word, "animosity." I found it to mean, "To have ill will or enmity toward another." So, if there had been generational enmity between father and son, this meant that there was an unwillingness to reconcile their differences. This meant that neither was willing to admit they were wrong, ask forgiveness, change, and restore the relationship.

Wow! These were exactly the feelings my son and I had to battle in the midst of our arguments. Sure, we needed to work through our disagreements, but we didn't need the extra influence from the generational iniquity making it more difficult.

When I shared this insight with my wife, she confirmed it, as she was aware of animosities between father and son on her family's side. So, as a representative of her family line, she confessed these iniquities. I also prayed through the stories of father-son animosities that I knew from my family history. I lastly acknowledged instances in my own life between me and my father.

I then asked the Lord, "When did this generational animosity start?" At that time, the Lord didn't show me anything. So over the next several weeks I kept asking the Lord while I waiting for insight.

Several weeks later, the Lord revealed to me where the iniquity of animosity started. He showed me a scene in my mind of a father and son who had gotten into a dispute. At some point, they closed off their hearts to one another, refusing to speak. The son felt deeply hurt, since he didn't feel heard. I could see them both standing there with their arms crossed and backs turned to each other, refusing to make things right. Life went on, and they did nothing to reconcile their differences. As I reflected on this scene, I could feel their animosity and hurt, which allowed me to identify their decisions to withdraw and curse one another in their hearts.

So, in prayer, I confessed this generational iniquity of animosity between father and son, while renouncing their decisions. Although the son did have a role in this iniquity, it was more the father's responsibility to initiate reconciliation. Thus, it was important that I, as the father, took initiative in prayer and reconciliation.

Soon after I had prayed, a change took place in the dynamic between my son and me. The very next time we got into a discussion, I felt I had more self-control and was less defensive. I could think more clearly and direct our conversation in positive ways. At first, my son was still a bit guarded, since he had learned to anticipate getting into an argument. But soon, he changed as he felt the influence no longer coming over us. Since then, we have been able to communicate better, have meaningful discussions, and resolve any arguments in healthier ways.

Visit

Wherever the Bible states that the iniquities of the fathers will visit the subsequent generations, the Hebrew word for "visit" or "visiting" is *paqad*[15]. It simply means, "to visit." It is the same as someone coming to your home, coming inside, and spending time with you.

In Genesis 21:1, the Lord visited Sarah. In Genesis 50:24-25, Joseph encouraged his family members by telling them that, someday, the Lord would visit them so as to bring them out of the land of Egypt. In each of these examples, the word *paqad* is used. The purpose of the visit can be either positive or negative. This is the same word used when a generational iniquity visits.

What my son and I experienced was a visit from a generational iniquity. This visitation came upon us whenever he and I got into a disagreement. This is exactly how a visitation from a generational iniquity functions. It's an influence that comes upon us in a particular situation, unannounced and uninvited, attempting to sway our thinking. Such a visitation most often occurs when we are in a similar circumstance to when one of our ancestors committed their sin that developed into iniquity.

When iniquities tempt, motivate or influence us to act in the same manner as our ancestors, it isn't as if we have no choice and, therefore, must comply. Rather, it is as though a familiar way of thinking and responding shifts into gear. Often, it will run parallel to an area in life where one already struggles, making it more difficult to overcome. Recognizing this helps to provide clues to the conditions that surrounded the generational iniquity, which need to be identified and prayed though.

There is an interesting observation I have made whenever a generational iniquity visits. Rarely, in the moment, do we recognize it as a visitation of generational iniquity. Even after all these years of experience, I still get caught off guard when one occurs. I find myself blaming the person or circumstance that triggered my negative response, while not even considering the possibility of generational iniquity. In the moment, the problem appears to be what is happening at hand -

---

[15] paqad *[Italicize Greek word]* (פקד), pronounced pâqad (*paw-kad'*), [H6285] ibid Strong's

45

what I see with our eyes. While focusing on that, I remain unaware that it is something historical that is influencing me. (Yet I have noticed that the time it takes me to consider and recognize something as a generational influence is much quicker than it used to be.)

Often, our sinful ways of responding are all too familiar to us, as if it is "normal" for us or for our family to react in a certain ways. As a result, we may not question our responses. And, even if we do consider that perhaps some sort of outside negative influence is affecting us, we may not have considered generational iniquity as the source. But now that we know about generational influences, we can consider them as a possibility.

By the way, a generational iniquity is not a demon. In some instance a demon might be associated with a generational iniquity. If there is a demon associated with a generational iniquity, keep in mind that it is there only to aggravate the existing influence of the iniquity in an attempt to tempt others to sin, so as to perpetuate the generational iniquity. The problem isn't so much the demonic but rather the generational iniquity. Demons are attracted to the iniquity. If you get rid of the iniquity through confession, the demon no longer have legal ground to stay, so it has to go too. At this point you simple tell the demon to leave in Jesus' name.

Visiting Can Be Negative Consequences
Numbers 14 tells the story of when "all the children of Israel murmured against Moses and Aaron" (v. 2) after the spies brought back a report about the Promised Land. When Joshua attempted to dissuade the people from their rebellion against God, they wanted to stone him.

God then spoke to Moses, expressing His tremendous frustration with the people and telling him that He was about to destroy them. As Moses had done several times before, he interceded with God on behalf of the people, regarding their iniquity. In prayer, Moses recalled God's character and reminded Him of His promises as he quoted Exodus 34:6-7. In

46

doing this, Moses was appealing to God to forgive "the iniquity of this people."

Despite the people having witnessed when God did amazing things, they still made a chose to respond in a sinful manner as they had done before (with exception of Joshua and Caleb). Their iniquity was that they had tested God and didn't listen to His voice nor did they trust Him. Ten times they did this! Despite God's attempts to teach them to respond differently, they chose not to change. Instead, they made their sinful response a way of life, and thus, it became an iniquity.

God then made it clear what the consequence would be. They were to suffer by wandering in the desert for forty years, and the parents would die during that time, never to enter the Promised Land. The children suffered as well, as a consequence of their parents' iniquities.

The children's time in the desert was an opportunity to learn to resist and overcome their parents' iniquities of murmuring and rebellion. This was required of them before going into the Promised Land. God didn't want to send warriors to conquer the land who, at the first sign of difficulty, would complain and spread dissension, and then would retreat and not trust their commander. If any break in the ranks occurred, the whole group would suffer. And they would most likely blame God and His leaders (as their forefathers did to Moses and Aaron) when it was clearly their own fault.

Suffering often accompanies the visiting of a generational iniquity. When those in leadership make decisions, those under them experience the outcome of those decisions, good or bad. Though God made it clear that the children wouldn't suffer the same fate as their parents who murmured and rebelled, they would have to wander in the desert until their parents died before they could enter the Promised Land. Though the children did suffer as a consequence of their parent's iniquities, they weren't being punished. Their suffering wasn't punitive. Rather, it was a cleansing, so as to remove the ways and bad habits of their parents, replacing them with godly character.

This suffering from generational iniquity is described as a "bearing," as in, "carrying a burden." It's like a load that is being carried that makes living life heavier at times than it should have been.

We are designed to carry loads in life. These loads are things such as responsibilities, tasks, work, trials, care for our family and others, and the like. They help us grow, to become mature and develop character. Yet, sometimes we have our regular loads, plus additional ones. These extra burdens are sometimes ones we have taken on, or sometimes they have been imposed upon us by life or by others. That is why Jesus said, "Come to Me, all who are weary and heavy-laden, and I will give you rest ... For My yoke is easy and My burden is light" (Matthew 11:28, 30). Jesus didn't say that He would free us from all burdens. But He did say that the burden He gives us is light in comparison.

Leviticus 26:39 says that the children will "pine away,"[16] not only for their own iniquities, but also for their fathers'. Lamentations 5:7 speaks of them bearing their forefathers' iniquities. Those who have bore generational iniquities have felt this way. It is like they are under something, like an oppression or weight that affects their quality of life.

If I have a bad habit of being late and justify speeding in my car, there is a chance that, one day, I will get a speeding ticket. And if that happens, and consequently I miss my daughter's dance performance, the speeding ticket is my punishment. However, missing her performance is a consequence, not a punishment. My daughter experiencing disappointment because I was late is also consequence. But she isn't being punished. In addition, my family might have to go without something for one month because I have to pay the speeding ticket. This too is a consequence that, unfortunately, they have to endure. But they aren't being punished. Because of my speeding, resulting in a speeding ticket, my whole family suffers.

America has a national debt because of decisions made by previous (as well as present) leaders. Though many of us didn't

---

[16] maqaq (מקק) - A primitive root; to melt; figuratively to flow, dwindle, vanish: - consume away, be corrupt, dissolve, pine away.

contribute to this debt, nor did we have a say about going into debt, all of us as citizens bear the consequences of it. This isn't unlike the iniquities of the fathers visiting the children.

Take, for instance, when my son and I were struggling with animosity. Our experience wasn't our punishment for what our ancestors had done. Instead, we were suffering the consequence of their choices, making our communication more difficult than it needed to be. Challenging as this was, we had a choice. We could either give in to it, or we could resist it. Until the influence lifted, we suffered under it. However, the suffering built character in our lives. We learned how to persevere, to reconcile and to do the right thing even if we didn't feel like it. And eventually, it paid off!

The Bible makes it clear that each person will be punished for his or her own wrongs committed (Ezekiel 18:20, Romans 2:6), unless they are confessed and repented of. The children will be punished for their own wrongs committed against God, while the fathers will be punished for theirs. Though the children may suffer because of what the parents have done, neither are punished on behalf of the other.

Estate and Genetic Inheritance

While generational iniquity is inherited, it is inherited differently than one from an estate as well as from one's genes.

An inheritance from an estate involves inheriting the tangible things our parents had accumulated throughout their lives. Until then, all of these items belong to our parents. So, as long as they are alive, our parents continue to add to, or subtract from, what we and our siblings will one day receive. Normally, an estate inheritance is distributed through a written will, which states the parents' exact instructions.

If generational iniquity were like an estate inheritance, we wouldn't inherit it until our parents died. In addition, our parents would have a say in how, when, or if it were to be distributed at all. But with generational iniquity, we receive it even while our parents are alive, and we have no say in how it is to be distributed.

49

Generational iniquity is also inherited differently than genetic inheritance. In some instances, generational iniquity may affect one's genes, but it isn't transferred genetically. When it comes to our genetic traits, each gene we inherited from our parents was there at our conception. From then on, we can't receive any additional or alternate genes or traits from them. If inheriting generational iniquity were like our genetic inheritance, any iniquities our parents committed after our conception wouldn't affect us. Likewise, any iniquities our grandparents committed after our parents and we were born would have no effect upon us as well. If this were true, we would be limited to inheriting only those generational iniquities committed by our parents up to the point of our conception.

But, Numbers 14 illustrates that we inherit generational iniquities regardless of the time of our conception or when the iniquity was committed. In this event, the children were affected by their parents' iniquities even though they were committed years after their children's conceptions.

The Bible makes it clear that the only condition for inheriting a generational iniquity is simply our ancestors committing the iniquity and not repenting from that iniquity. It makes no difference whether a generational iniquity occurred before or after we were conceived. What is true is that, if left unconfessed, it has the potential to visit its influence upon us and subsequent generations.

Things to Consider

- Looking back, when were some times that you think you may have been visited by a generational iniquity?
- What were some characteristics of those times that indicate it was from a generational iniquity?
- What would you do differently, knowing what you know now about how generational iniquities visit us?
- In what ways do you think you may be suffering due to a generational iniquity? How do you think God would have you respond and live your life in regard to it?

50

Visiting the Generations

*...visiting the iniquity of the fathers
upon the children,
and upon the children's children,
unto the third and to the fourth generation.
Exodus 37:4*

Always Left Behind

any years ago, I went through a time of burnout. I was exhausted, both mentally and emotionally. It took me about three years to begin to feel somewhat normal again. During my recovery from burnout, it continued to be a difficult and lonely time. Prior to the burnout, I had poured out a tremendous amount of energy into my work for many years. And now, I was exhausted and spent. The burnout had caused me to feel used and forgotten. I felt as if I was an orange, and God had squeezed all the juice out of me. And, since I had no more to give, He no longer needed me. So He moved on, finding someone else He could use. I knew this wasn't true, but I couldn't shake the feeling.

While in burnout, I struggled with jealousy and anger. This would often occur whenever I saw others who were successful and seemed to be getting ahead in life. I felt it was unfair. They got to move forward while I was being left behind. They got to be successful while I only got to survive. I felt stuck, as if this predicament would never change for the rest of my life.

In the midst of this, I tried my best to be excited for others and not to say hurtful things. Despite how miserable I felt, I would attempt to bless others and thank God for what He was doing in their lives. This did help minimize my depression. Nevertheless, despite my efforts, the pain of feeling that "I will always be left behind" didn't go away.

So I went to see a friend and shared my struggle. We asked the Lord to show us if there was a root cause to the belief: "I will always be left behind." As we listened, the Lord indicated that it was related to something generational.

As I continued to listen, the Lord showed me in my mind what had happened. When my ancestors had migrated across the United States in a horse-drawn wagon, they were carrying a baby with them. But, due to certain circumstances, they decided it was best to leave the child behind. The plan was to have someone else bring the child six months later when they would complete the journey. This arrangement was carried out very matter-of-factly, with no consoling of the child. The Lord revealed that the child felt abandoned – left behind. As I saw this, I could feel the pain of the child rising up in me, and the words, "I will always be left behind!" came right out of my mouth. Somehow, I knew in my spirit that this was what my great-great-grandfather had felt. I began to cry as I felt his pain.

So, in prayer, I told the whole story as the Lord had revealed it to me. I confessed the bitterness of my great-great-grandfather while renouncing his decision of: "I will always be left behind." I also forgave my ancestors for treating him the way they did, whether their hurting him was intentional or not.

After I prayed, the depression I had been under lifted off of me. Even though my circumstances hadn't immediately changed, my internal response toward them did. I stopped feeling intense depression. I no longer struggled with thoughts of "I will always be left behind," whenever I was around those who seemed successful. As a result, this tremendously helped in my recovery from burnout.

With regard to a family line, one generation consists of the children of a common parent. So, my children would be the next generation after me. Exodus 34:7 clearly states that the iniquities of the fathers visit the first, second, third, and fourth generations. Even though only the first four generations are mentioned in this verse, this by no means excludes any generations beyond the fourth from being influenced as well. In addition, all it takes is someone in a subsequent generation to recommit the same generational iniquity, and then it is perpetuated for the future generations.

Exodus 20:5, Numbers 14:18 and Deuteronomy 5:9 reiterate what Exodus 34:7 says. These verses all speak of the "visiting of the iniquities of the fathers upon the children, unto the third and the fourth generation." The Hebrew word for "children" is often used to refer to any of the descendants of a father, which includes grandchildren and so on. There are many times in the Bible when the word "children" doesn't just refer to the next generation, but also to subsequent generations. Ben-Ammi is referred to as: "the father of the children of Ammon, to this day" (Genesis 19:38). Throughout Israel's history, no matter how many generations removed, the descendants are referred to as: "the children of Israel" (Exodus 3:15).

I have seen instances when three generations had decided not to be like their ancestors. The grandparents initiated this change by becoming Christians, deciding to live godly lives, and not participating in any of the sinful ways of their forefathers. They then raised their children this way, who did the same with their children. Much to their credit, this did make a difference by sowing godly character into the family line. However, they were still visited by generational iniquities. But once they prayed through the iniquities, they entered into even more blessing.

Unfortunately, some families may have had a horrible elder family member. This individual may have made life very hard and miserable for others. So when that person died, this did bring great relief for many. In part, this is true, for this person can no longer cause havoc. But that person's death didn't stop the influence of the iniquities that person committed. And therefore, these need to be addressed in prayers of confession.

53

Scriptural Examples of Generational Iniquity Visiting

In the Bible, there are many examples of generational iniquities. These are times when an iniquity from one family member manifested in subsequent generations. Some examples can be found in the lives of Abraham and his descendants.

Abraham's Family Line

The following chart displays a portion of Abraham's family line as found in the book of Genesis. It starts with Abraham's father and extends to Abraham's grandchildren[17].

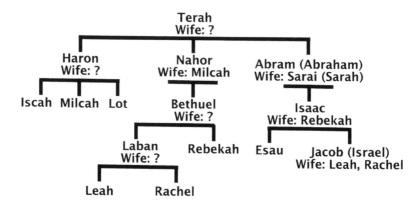

Anytime someone comes into God's family, choosing to follow and obey Him, there are inevitably some areas in that person's life that need to be cleaned up. People bring with them their personal and family issues, which include iniquities and areas of ignorance about God's ways. Each family has its own unique traits and patterns of iniquity that need to be addressed.

When we read about Abraham's family in the book of Genesis, we definitely see this. We need to remember that when God first spoke to him, Abraham had no apparent upbringing of God and His ways. The Torah (the first five books of the Bible) hadn't been written yet. But, as a faithful Father, God took Abraham and his family members through

---

[17] Abraham's name was Abram before God changed it to Abraham (Gen. 17:5). Sarah's name was Sarai before God changed it to Sarah (Gen. 17:15). Jacob's name was changed to Israel by God (Gen. 32:28).

various experiences to shape them. He used various trials and circumstances to confront and uproot negative family dynamics. When we look at Abraham's family line, we see several of these dynamics, which had become generational iniquities. The three that stand out the most are: passivity, deception and manipulation.

Passivity

Passivity is something with which Abraham, Isaac and Jacob all struggled (father, son and grandson). Ironically, in identical situations, Abraham and Isaac both responded in the same manner, acting passively and out of fear, instead of courage, honor, and faith (see Genesis 12:10-13; 20:1-2; 26:1-7). In every instance, they acted out of fear for their lives instead of facing their fear and trusting God.

Twice, Abraham dishonored his wife by failing to protect her. He was passive. Instead of telling others that Sarah was his wife, he said she was his sister,[18] instructing her to do the same the same thing. He did this out of fear for his life, instead of being willing to proclaim Sarah as his wife even if it meant forfeiting his own life.

Yet, Abraham had no reason to do what he did. For the Lord had spoken twice to him before this incident, promising that He would bless him (Genesis 12:2-3; 12:7). Having such a promise should have reassured Abraham that it wasn't time for him to die, since he hadn't yet had a son. This was all the more reason for him to stand up for Sarah, making it clear to everyone that she was indeed his wife. Instead, he lied, thinking only to save his own life, even if it meant sacrificing his wife. Thus, he missed an opportunity to walk by faith by trusting God.

One thing I love about the Lord is that He will bring about in us what He intends, even despite our weaknesses and shortcomings. The Lord was gracious. Abraham's life was spared despite both his lack of faith and Pharaoh's anger when Pharaoh found out Abraham had lied.

---

[18] Sarah is actually Abraham's half-sister, as they share the same father but not the same mother (Genesis 20:12).

Yet, one would think that Abraham would have learned his lesson. But when the second opportunity to get it right came along, he acted just as he had before (Genesis 20).

Even though Abraham hadn't trusted God either time, the Lord remained faithful and was gracious to him. For, even afterwards, He reminded Abraham again and again of His promises to him (Genesis 13:14-18, 15:1-20, 17:1-21, 18:10-13).

Despite all of this, there were still consequences. Abraham's actions resulted in trouble and distrust between him and those to whom he lied. And one has to only wonder how much Sarah did not feel cherished because of what Abraham had done, by not standing up for her.[19]

Ironically, many years later, Isaac did the same thing to his wife (Rebecca) as his father Abraham had done (Genesis 26:1-7). This is how generational iniquity works. When in a situation similar to that of to his father, Isaac was tempted to respond in the same manner. Though Isaac had never witnessed the times when his father had been afraid for his life, he found himself tempted in the same way. Unfortunately, instead of resisting it, he also responded in passivity by not protecting his wife. He even said the very same lie about his wife that his father had: "She is my sister" (Genesis 26:7-9)!

Then, along came Jacob, Abraham's grandson through Isaac, who inherited the same generational tendency to be passive. Keep in mind that one's circumstances don't have to be exactly the same as one's ancestors - just similar - in order for the generational influences to visit. In Jacob's case, it only needed to be an opportunity to be passive. Even so, he was not bound nor obligated to respond in the same manner even though he may have felt tempted to do so.

---

[19] Perhaps, the Lord's way of ministering to Sarah's heart was by changing her name. Prior to both events, her name was Sarai, which means, "dominutive." But, one day, the Lord changed her name to Sarah, which means "princess." To the Lord, she was more than just a woman with authority. She was a princess, too! It was as if He were saying to Sarah, "Though your husband may not have treated you as a princess, I see you as a one. And so you shall, for you '...shall be a mother of nations'" (Genesis 17:15-16).

One day, Jacob was facing a situation where he had to make a decision. He was about to face his brother Esau, who was going to kill him, and Jacob was afraid for his life. He had two choices: he could be like the previous two generations, attempting to save his life at the expense of his loved ones. Or, he could risk his own life for their sake. So, despite his fear, he chose to resist the generational iniquity of passivity. He faced his brother, instead of submitting to his fear. He put his own life at risk, thus protecting his wives. As a result, he broke the family trait of passivity. Something changed in Jacob that day, which is discussed in more detail in the chapter titled, "Wrestling."

Deception

When we read through the book of Genesis, it doesn't take long to notice that deception runs through Jacob's family line. It came through his mother, Rebekah. It also caused division between Jacob and his brother, Esau. This occurred when Jacob tricked Esau out of his birthright. At another time, Rebekah made a plan to deceive her own husband, Isaac, so Jacob could get his father's blessing that should have been Esau's. This created even more resentment from Esau toward Jacob.

After Jacob left home, the pattern of deception continued. Laban, who is Rebekah's brother, tricked Jacob on his wedding night. Jacob was promised Rachel's hand in marriage, but he ended up marrying Leah because Laban switched Rachel for Leah without Jacob knowing it until the next day. Laban did this despite that Jacob had fulfilled his part of the deal to earn the right to have Rachel as his wife. Over time, Laban also cheated Jacob by changing his wages ten times. Later on, Jacob tricked his uncle out of most of his livestock.

And it didn't stop there...

One day when Jacob decided to secretly leave his uncle out of fear of him. Laban pursued him. When he found Jacob, he accused Jacob, saying, "Why did you run off secretly and deceive me?" (Genesis 31:27). He also accused Jacob of stealing his idols. Ironically, it was Rachel who had stolen the idols. To keep from being searched, she lied, telling everyone that she couldn't get down from her camel for personal reasons. In reality, she was sitting on top of the stolen idols.

It makes one wonder what other acts of deception these family members committed against one another that aren't even recorded. As always happens in such cases, each time there is deception, it produces a big mess of suspicions, mistrust, accusations, resentments and family division. Deception was a way of life for Jacob's family. It was a family trait, iniquity. They not only had made a habit of it, but also they accused one another of doing it.

Keep in mind that Laban and Rebekah were brother and sister, coming from the same parents. The Bible doesn't say how their parents lived their lives. But as is characteristic of a generational iniquity, there is a good chance that being deceptive was a character trait of at least one of their parents, and possibly that of previous generations. Somewhere it started, it became a way of life, and no one bothered to put an end to address it.

The generational iniquity of deception didn't stop with Jacob. Many years later, Jacob's own sons acted "deceitfully as they spoke to Shechem" (Genesis 34:13). They used deception in order to exact revenge. Indeed, what Shechem had done was awful (he assaulted Jacob's daughter, Dinah), deserving of punishment. Yet, they should have sought God first as to what they should have done. Instead, their first impulse, like their ancestors, was to act deceitfully, luring Shechem and his family into a false sense of security before attacking and looting their city.

Manipulation

When we try to fulfill, through our own efforts and striving, what God has promised He will do, these actions are manipulations on our part. What God promises, we don't have to make happen. Our part is to have faith and to cooperate with His plan, not to manipulate people and circumstances in order to make sure God's promises come true. The end doesn't justify the means. Yet, this trait of manipulation is observed in Abraham's family.

Isaac and Ishmael were sons of Abraham. Concerning faith versus works, Isaac is often referred to as, "The son of promise," while Ishmael is referred to as, "The son of works." Isaac was the result of God fulfilling His promise to Abraham, requiring Abraham by faith to trust God to fulfill His promise. On the other hand, Ishmael was the result of Abraham attempting to fulfill God's promise by his own efforts and manipulation.

The Lord had promised Abraham that He would give him and Sarah a son through their union. But, as they saw themselves getting old, instead of trusting God to make it happen, they decided to take matters into their own hands. So, through their own efforts and manipulation, Abraham had a son (Ishmael) through Hagar, thinking that somehow this would fulfill what God had promised.

By the way, this instance was yet another time when Abraham was passive. Even though Sarah insisted that he have relations with Hagar, Abraham didn't have to. He had a choice. Evidently, Sarah was struggling at this time with her own faith concerning God's promise to them. What she actually needed was for her husband to be strong for both of them and to say, "No! We need to trust the Lord."

But yet God was gracious. Once again, despite their manipulation, God kept His promise, and one day, they had Isaac.

Many years later, Isaac got married. When he was about to become a father, the Lord gave him a promise concerning the twins in his wife's (Rebekah's) womb. God said, "The older will serve the younger" (Genesis 25:23). But, instead of trusting God to see how He would fulfill this promise, Isaac gave in to familiar family trait of manipulation.

When the twins were born, the older was named Esau, and the younger was named Jacob. What is ironic is that Jacob's name means "heel catcher" or "supplanter," meaning "one who wrongfully or illegally seizes and holds the place of another." He was named Jacob because, after Esau came out, Jacob was "grasping Esau's heel" (Genesis 25:26). Keep in mind, the Lord didn't tell Isaac and Rebekah what to name their children. He only told them what would become of them. But, coming from a family line of manipulators, they apparently interpreted Jacob's grasping of Esau's heel as an act of manipulation. So, they named him thus, Jacob.

It makes one wonder how Jacob was affected every time he heard his name, let alone when he was told the story of his birth and of how he got his name. One can imagine how this would put an expectation upon him, that he would be a manipulator throughout his life.

As we know, Jacob did live up to his name. When his brother was starving, instead of showing kindness, Jacob manipulated him into giving up his birthright for a bowl of lentils. Yes, Esau was foolish, but Jacob didn't have to do what he did.

Even though it was wrong, was Jacob only acting as was expected of him when he tricked his brother? Did he think to himself, "Someday, my brother is going to serve me, so I have to make it happen"? Jacob's actions demonstrated that he believed he had to manipulate his circumstances in order to get results.

Keeping with the family trait, Rebekah and Jacob acted manipulatively when they tricked Isaac into giving his blessing to Jacob, as we discussed earlier (also see Genesis 27). Though the blessing legally should have gone to Esau, the firstborn, Jacob consented to Rebekah's plan to manipulate Isaac in order to fulfill the promise that Jacob would rule over Esau.

Again, Jacob didn't have to play along with his mother's plan. He could have said, "No Mom. I don't want to be a part of this." But instead, he gave into the generational influence of: "This is what we do: we manipulate the situation to make sure things happen."

What if Rebekah had done nothing? What if she had sought the Lord, acknowledged her doubts, and trusted Him instead? If she had, she would have seen the Lord fulfill His promise, despite the circumstances and her tendency to manipulate. In addition, Jacob wouldn't have learned how to be a manipulator.

He would have seen the Lord come through without their interference, and he would have learned to trust the Lord.

And what if Jacob had never manipulated his brother and father? What if he had trusted the Lord and thought, "Wow! As impossible as this situation seems in light of God's promise, I wonder how He will fulfill His promise! Though I am tempted to manipulate, I will wait and see!" We can only imagine what God would have done. Jacob would have learned that God can fulfill His promises without anyone needing to manipulate the situation.

And what about what the name Jacob's parents gave him? In light of God's promise and His character, they should have given him a name that means "leader," "over-comer" or, "God fulfills His word" – not, "supplanter." This only confirms that the influence of one's generational iniquities tends to color how one interprets one's experiences and expectations of the future. It also influences how one sees God. In their case, their view of God was: "Whatever promises God makes, we have to make sure they happen."

Despite all this, the Lord correctly saw Jacob for who he was to be. Many years later, God corrected Isaac's and Rebekah's error by changing Jacob's name to Israel, which means: "struggles with God." This is because Jacob "struggled with God and men and [overcame]" (Genesis 32:28).

The Lord is faithful. He doesn't need our help to fulfill His promises. He only wants us to trust Him. Know that despite our passivity, deceptions and manipulations, He will make sure that His plans, purposes and promises will be fulfilled!

Remember that manipulation of your circumstances is a demonstration of your lack of faith in the Lord, since you are insisting that you must intervene. Cooperation with the Lord is a demonstration of your faith in Him that He is in control despite your circumstances. Trust Him and know that He will do great things!

Having shared all of this, I would like to put in a good word for Abraham. As we can see, he didn't start off as a great man of faith. But through his mistakes, he learned about God's ways and His character. As a result, he became a man of faith. The same is with each of us. For the Lord is making us into men and women of faith in Him. Now, "It is those who are of faith who are sons of Abraham" (Galatians 3:7), and, "If you belong to Christ, then you are Abraham's descendants, heirs according to promise" (Galatians 3:29).

What I appreciate so much about Abraham and his family line is that their stories give great hope to people like you and me. That, despite our foolishness and crazy family dynamics, the Lord will work His plan in and through us. And, as we trust in Him and cooperate with Him, He will see Him do extraordinary things.

Things to Consider

- What are some other possible generational iniquities that you've seen in the Bible?
- What are some dynamics you've noticed in your family that might be generational iniquities? What stories or events have led you to think so?
- What are some possible generational iniquities you see in others? What stories or events have led you to think so?
- What are some words or promises that the Lord has given you?
- If you are still waiting, how have you been tempted to fulfill those words yourself?
- What negative traits is the Lord trying to put to death in you as you wait for Him to fulfill His words in your life? Could these be family line traits?

Undoing Generational Iniquity

But He was wounded for our transgressions,
He was bruised for our iniquities:
the chastisement of our peace was upon Him;
and with His stripes we are healed....
...and He bare the sin of many.
Isaiah 53:5, 12 ^{KJV}

Utter Destruction and Despair

Jane suffered from horrible nightmares. They were terrifying. What made them worse was that she had them ever week, and she couldn't stop them from reoccurring. These nightmares affected her sleep, which left her exhausted throughout the day. She had been having them for so long that they had become just a "normal" part of her life. Since she didn't know what to do about them, she had resigned herself to just suffer through them.

Her nightmares all had a common theme: utter destruction and despair. There was great hopelessness, with a strong sense that nothing could be done to turn back the destruction. It was like an unstoppable flood.

As there were many issues in Jane's childhood that had this theme, she took the time to pray through them first. When we sought the the Lord for further insight, He indicated that this theme of "utter destruction and despair" was rooted in generational issues as well. So Jane and I asked the Lord to show us where this all started.

The Lord gave us a picture of a peaceful village. There was music, calmness and no apparent fears. At first, this didn't make sense, since the scene didn't have anything to do with destruction and despair. So, we asked the Lord for further insight.

He showed Jane the image of a little girl who lived in the village. The little girl was Jane's ancestor. One day, the village was invaded. When Jane saw this, she began to feel the utter terror of the little girl and the people as the land was flooded with invaders. There were so many invaders who came so suddenly that there was no way of stopping them. It was like a flood. As the little girl watched in terror, she could do nothing as she saw her people mercilessly slaughtered before her own eyes. She saw her village destroyed. She was removed from her homeland and made into a slave. As a slave, she was greatly mistreated and abused. In the midst of all her hurt, she became bitter and resentful over everything that had happened. And, out her hatred, she made many awful and negative decisions.

The Lord then revealed to me something I didn't expect. He showed me that I had ancestors who had invaded the little girl's village. In that moment, I felt the awfulness of what they had done. So I looked at Jane and said, "It was we who did this to you." And when I did, Jane immediately said, "Yes, it was!"

God allowed us to identify with our ancestors in order to bring about reconciliation and healing! This allowed Jane to share all the hurt and anger she was bearing of her ancestors. When she was ready, I, as a representative of my ancestors, confessed as wrong to Jane that what my ancestors had done, asking for her forgiveness. She forgave. I also confessed to the Lord the iniquities of my ancestors.

Jane then spent time praying through all that had happened to her ancestor, the little girl, confessing her decisions and forgiving those who had wronged her and her people. She also renounced any decisions her ancestor had made in response to this horrible historical event.

As a result, the nightmares stopped. Jane has not had any more bad dreams with the theme of utter destruction and despair. This has greatly helped her ability to sleep, allowing her to be more rested and, thus, less tired throughout her days. She no longer just has to suffer through them!

Isaiah 53 is a prophecy of when Jesus would suffer and die on the Cross. And, when He did, He took on all of our sins, transgressions, and iniquities. As you read through Isaiah 53, notice that all three Hebrew words for "sin," "transgression" and "iniquity" are used:[20]

Sin (*chatta'ah*)
> Verse 10: "He hath put Him to grief: when Thou shalt make His soul an offering for sin…"
> Verse 12: "He bore the sin of many…"

Transgression (*pasha*)
> Verse 5: "But He was wounded for our transgressions… "
> Verse 8: "…for the transgression of my people was He stricken."

Iniquity (*avon*)
> Verse 5: "He was bruised for our iniquities..."
> Verse 6: "…the LORD hath laid on Him the iniquity of us all."
> Verse 11: "…for He shall bear their iniquities."

On the Cross, Jesus fulfilled, once and for all, all of the Old Testament sacrifices that the priests were required to perform (Hebrews 7:26-28). He was made a sin offering. He took the punishment for our transgressions. And, just like the scapegoat (Leviticus 16:21), Jesus bore our iniquities!

Isaiah 53:5 says that, "He was bruised for our iniquities." Mark 14:65 tells of one of the times when Jesus was bruised. "Some began to spit at Him, and to blindfold Him, and to beat Him with their fists, and to say to Him, 'Prophesy!' And the officers received Him with slaps in the face."

Jesus' death on the Cross fulfilled what was required for all of our sins, transgressions and iniquities – past, present and future! Yet, it was we who committed such things, and

---

[20] These verses from Isaiah 53 are quoted from the KJV translation.

therefore, it was we who should have received eternal death. But through Jesus, our debts are paid!

Becoming a Christian means recognizing that we are sinful, and that we need Jesus as our Lord and Savior, thus receiving, by faith, what He did for us. This is called salvation, saving us from eternal separation from God. As a result, when we die in this life, we will have eternal life with God. We are saved by believing on the Lord, Jesus Christ (Acts 16:13), not by confessing all of our sins or by any good deeds we could ever perform (Ephesians 2:8-9). But while becoming a Christian saves us from eternal death, it doesn't stop the reaping of what we and our ancestors sowed.

Once we become saved, we then become recipients of the benefits of our salvation through Jesus. However, we must actively participate in the Lord's work in our lives. Confessing our sins is one of the ways we participate. As I previously explained, our sins set in motion the reaping of bad fruit in our lives. When we confess our sins, this stops the reaping of those sins. The same is true of transgressions and iniquities.

It is like having a bank account in your own name. God anticipated that throughout your life you would accumulate debts because of your sins, and these debts you could never pay. So out of His great love for you, He made a deposit on your behalf to cover these debts. Yet, even though this account is full, you will never experience the benefits of it unless you make withdrawals. This is done by confession of sins. By becoming a Christian, you have access to this "account."

By the way, if you have not already done so and would like to become a Christian, turn to the back of the book to learn how. In this way, you can be a recipient of what Jesus did.

When Jesus' disciples asked how they should pray, Jesus provided an example known as "the Lord's Prayer." Part of it includes asking God for forgiveness of our sins. Luke 11:4 says: "And forgive us our sins, for we ourselves also forgive everyone who is indebted to us." Note: we are also to forgive (releasing any indebtedness) those who have sinned against us.

I John 1:9 says, "If we confess our sins, He is faithful and righteous to forgive us our sins and to cleanse us from all unrighteousness." The reason we confess our sins is so God can cleanse us from the unrighteousness of our sins, and thus applying to us what Jesus did on the cross.

James 5:16 says, "Therefore, confess your sins to one another, and pray for one another so that you may be healed. The effective prayer of a righteous man can accomplish much."

Confessing our sins is part of our spiritual hygiene. It is something we need to do on a regular basis as Christians. It is for our benefit. As we go through life, we unfortunately sin from time to time. And, whether we do so intentionally or not, we still need to confess our sins.

As we mature as Christians, we learn more about God's ways. In the process, we often discover sins that we were unaware of or had forgotten. This is true of generational iniquities as well. When the Lord reveals these to us, we are to confess them so we may experience the benefits of doing so.

Generational Representatives

God originally designed us to inherit the blessings and good character sown by our ancestors. But when sin entered the world, the influences of generational iniquities became our inheritance as well. In addition, we inherit generational iniquities regardless of whether we have sinned in the same manner as our ancestors.

Daniel understood this. He prayed regularly to the Lord concerning the iniquities of his ancestors, for he knew that it was because of their iniquities, the nation of Israel was in captivity in Babylon. What is important to note is that when he prayed, he said, "We have sinned" not, "I confess that they sinned." Because he was a descendant of those who had committed the iniquities, Daniel had the authority, as a representative, to confess their iniquities. In addition, he could also represent his nation as he was an Israelite.

The significance of confessing generational iniquities is seen in Daniel's life. The enemy knew the impact of Daniel's prays and how they would help set the nation of Israel free. Thus, the enemy attempted to stop him from praying by devising a plan to have Daniel thrown into the lions' den. But despite this, the Lord delivered Daniel and honored his prayers of confessing the generational iniquities of his ancestors. For when it was time, the Lord set the Israelites free from their captivity in Babylon and restored them to the land of Israel.

Just like Daniel, we can do the same. As representatives of our ancestors, we have the privilege of confessing inherited iniquities, and thus, putting an end to the visitation of the negative influences.

The following are instances in the Bible when others confessed the iniquities of their ancestors, leaders, and their own people: Exodus 34:8-9; Leviticus 16:21, 26:40; II Chronicles 7:14; Ezra 9:6-15; Nehemiah 1:6-11, 9:1-2; Psalms 106:6; Jeremiah 3:25, 14:7, 20; Daniel 9:4-8ff, 20. By the way, Psalm 106 is primarily a confession of Israel's historical sins and iniquities.

Things to Consider

Before you consider addressing any generational sins, do the following concerning your personal sins.

- Recall a time when you confessed your sins to the Lord. What noticeable difference did it make for you?
- Stop for a moment and ask the Lord to show you any sins you may not be aware of but still need to confess.
  - Take the time, right now, and confess them to the Lord. If at all possible, find a trusted friend with whom you can do this. Pray for one another afterwards.
- Who are some people you need to forgive? In prayer, forgive these people. If needed, ask the Lord to help you forgive.
- What are some sins you struggle with that are similar to those of your family's generational iniquities?
  - Begin to confess your participation in these.
  - Ask the Lord to help you to overcome them.

68

Characteristics of Generational Iniquity

…you are doing just as your fathers did.
Acts 7:51

If You Venture Out, Bad Things Will Happen

Nick and Ester love to pray and intercede. They often pray for people, cities and nations. From time to time, the Lord has directed them to travel places around the world and pray at those locations. These "prayer trips" have been fruitful. Often, amazing things happened. But unfortunately, it was not without some sort of cost.

Almost without exception, whenever they went on one of their prayer trips, something bad would happen to their family. It even got to the point where their adult children became fearful, just knowing that their parents were about to go on another trip.

One time, their granddaughter almost drowned in their swimming pool, and for no apparent reason. Before one trip, their daughter almost got crushed between the car door and a lamppost. On another occasion, their son's car broke down several times, needing to be towed three times in just two weeks. Right before one trip, the cat ran away. Add to this that Nick and Ester would often find themselves getting into arguments a few days before leaving on a prayer trip. These are just a few examples of the type of things that would occur.

Now, it only seemed reasonable to conclude that Nick and Ester were experiencing spiritual warfare. They were being attacked by the enemy, because what they were doing for the Lord was strategic and effective. So the enemy was attempting to discourage them from going on such trips. The fact that their children were often targets was causing them to reconsider. Though they understood spiritual warfare, these attacks were especially excessive and consistent.

Nick and Ester attempted to keep their lives pure and would pray prior to going on these trips. Yet despite their efforts to minimize the attacks of the enemy, the attacks would still occur. So they thought that perhaps there was something else that made them so susceptible. What it was, they didn't know – at least not yet.

Together we asked the Lord to show us if there was anything that made Nick and Ester particularly vulnerable. The Lord indicated that it was generational. What He revealed to them was that one of Nick's ancestors suffered the loss of his eldest son, and he didn't want to ever risk losing his other son. So when his next son wanted to venture out, the father disapproved. He even threatened him in an attempt to discourage him. Instead of facing his fear, being honest and blessing his son, the father threatened him, saying, "If you do this, bad things will happen." In essence, he cursed any adventures and plans his son would consider to undertake.

The son was torn between wanting his father's approval versus desiring to venture out into the world, which was what he wanted and felt called to do. Eventually, he decided to step out and do what he wanted even if it resulted in his father's disapproval.

In Ester's family line, the Lord revealed that her great-grandfather had disapproved of his son's (Ester's grandfather's) desire to become a pastor. He was made to feel obligated to support everyone else at the expense of his own desires. This affected his ability to trust that God would provide. This, in turn, extinguished any desire to pursue his calling in life. Just like Nick's ancestor, Ester's grandfather didn't have his father's blessing. Yet, in this case, he gave up instead of pursuing what he wanted.

So in prayer, Nick retold the story of his ancestors, acknowledging the father's unwillingness to face his fear and to risk. He also confessed the father's cursing of his son. He then renounced the curse of, "If you venture out (step out into what you are called to do), bad things will happen." He also confessed any resentment the son had toward his father, renouncing the lies he believed, such as: "I can't get his approval" and "Bad things happen when you step out."

Next, Ester shared in prayer the story of her ancestors, how her great-grandfather had disapproved of her grandfather's desire to be a pastor. She confessed his disapproval and his withholding of blessing from his son. She also acknowledged any resentment that her grandfather had towards his father. She then renounced any negative decisions that her grandfather made, such as, "I will never do what I was called to do," "If I become a pastor, I won't be able to support everybody" and "God won't provide."

Weeks later, Nick and Ester took a risk and went on another prayer trip. They reported that nothing bad happened to their family! Their children were apprehensive at first because of past experiences. But they soon had peace once they realized that nothing bad happened.

Now, Nick and Ester can go on their prayer trips being more focused, not having to feel so concerned for their children. Their children have been blessed as well. And as a bonus, the family cat came back!

This experience demonstrates that sometimes, spiritual warfare is more than it needs to be. In this case, the enemy took advantage of historical generational iniquities, which left vulnerability in Nick and Ester's family. Once it was addressed, the intensity of the spiritual warfare dropped significantly!

Characteristics of Generational Iniquity

What distinguishes something as a generational iniquity? Before we jump to conclusions that something is being caused by a generational iniquity, it's a good idea to consider other possibilities. In some instances, what we are experiencing could be a combination of several causes. The following are some things to consider.

<u>Trials and Times of Testing</u> – These are challenging and difficult times in our life that the Lord has permitted in order to make us more like Christ (I Peter 4:12). During these times, He desires to bring out the best in us while attempting to rid us of the worst. Our responsibility during these periods is to cooperate with God in faith, prayer and obedience. Perseverance is often required.

<u>Spiritual Warfare</u> – We have an enemy (I Peter 5:8) who doesn't want to see us succeed in what God is accomplishing through us. Therefore, we need to be aware of his tactics, be prepared, minimize vulnerabilities and be on guard through the means God has given us (Ephesians 6:10-18). If we have any unconfesssed sin, this gives the enemy access to cause trouble in our lives. Therefore, it is always wise to keep our lives pure and to confess our sins.

<u>Our Flesh</u> – Our flesh motivates us to sin (Galatians 5:17). If we nurture our flesh, which is our own fault, it will bring enough trouble on its own. In addition, the enemy will use this to take advantage of us.

<u>Ignorance and Bad Decisions</u> – Sometimes there are natural consequences that occur when we make mistakes, do things out of ignorance or ignore wisdom (Proverbs 22:3).

<u>Suffering and Persecution</u> – Since we live in a fallen world, we experience suffering – whether directly, through people's choices, or indirectly, through changing circumstances. Depending upon the society we live in or the type of people we encounter, we may also suffer for being Christians (Matthew 5:10-11).

<u>Personal Neglect</u> – Lack of sleep and exercise, dehydration and poor nutrition can result in problems. Allergies, sicknesses and chemical imbalances also affect our feelings. Addictions, even mild ones, also affect us. I knew of a woman who thought her recent emotional difficulties were the result of something in her past. Instead, she was suffering from withdrawals from quitting coffee, which eventually went away.

<u>Bad Fruit from One's Past</u> – As shared in the chapter titled, *Dealing with Personal Root Causes*, some troubles in our lives are from unresolved issues from our past. If there is fruit, then there is a root (Galatians 6:7).

<u>God Ordained Seasons</u> - There are times throughout our our lives where God takes us through long challenging seasons, often evolving years. He does this in order to bring about His purposes in and through us. These seasons are opportunities required of you in order to make you more like Jesus. For more information about this, see my book titled: *Hey God, Are We There Yet?*[21]

As with most problems, if we are able to recognize what the real issue is, we can be better able to know what actions need to be taken. Otherwise, we may be looking for a cause that isn't there. Or, we will attempt to use a solution that does not apply. With regard to the influence of generational iniquities, the following are some key characteristics to look for:

Power to Influence – Does what you are experiencing seem to have an unusually strong power to influence? If so, what is the theme?

Patterns – Are there recurring patterns or certain situations in which the influence occurs? If so, what are some of the characteristics common to those situations?

Persistence – Do these patterns keep recurring despite your efforts to resist them? Do they persist despite your attempt to consider other possible causes and to apply the means to resolve them?

Previous Generations – Do you know of persons in previous generations who had similar experiences? Has the Lord indicated to you that the issue is related to something generational?

---

[21] *Hey God, Are We There Yet?*, ISBN: 978-0976354949

Power to Influence

The most obvious characteristic of a generational iniquity is its power to influence. This influence most often affects our thoughts, causing us to consider reacting in a certain manner. It compels us to give in to negative compulsions, rather than to do the right thing. In some cases, it feels as if we have no choice, when in reality, we do. We just don't like the oppression we are under at the time. So, in order to get out from under the duress, we often give in to the influence rather than endure it.

The influence skews thinking, motivating us to respond inappropriately, even though we know we should respond differently. Sometimes, the influence may be so strong that it makes it difficult to consider other ways of responding. At such times, it takes determination, choosing to make the right choice despite how one may feel.

One area where generational influence manifests is in our relationships, such as with our spouse, parents, children, friends, co-workers, bosses and acquaintances. It interferes with our interactions and responses with one another. For instance, it can affect our perception of men, women or authority figures, causing us to see them in a negative light or to anticipate negative behaviors from them. It can also interfere with how we see God. For example, we might know He is good, but for some unknown reason we can't shake the feeling that perhaps He isn't.

Generational influences can also show up in various aspects of our lives, such as finances, health, employment and opportunities. They have the ability hinder these things, so that things don't go well. They can cause our lives to become more difficult than they should be. It's as if life has more tasks, difficulties and challenges than it should.

An influence from a generational iniquity can be described as an unseen, felt, motivating force, coming from outside you, whereas, unresolved issues from your past tend to feel like an influence coming from within you. It's common not to initially recognize when the influence from a generational iniquity is visiting. It is easy to automatically assume that the present situation is the real reason for how you feel, and as if it is the sole source of the issue at hand. What makes it difficult to distinguish a generational iniquity from a stressful situation is that, if you have any unresolved issues with same theme, these will tend to be your primary focus. They will distract you from recognizing the influence of a generational iniquity. Therefore, the more past issues for your personal history (conception to now) you resolve, the more you will be able to identify whether an influence is the result of a generational iniquity.

Patterns

A generational iniquity has a pattern to it, recurring in particular settings or circumstances. This is similar to the bad fruit from unresolved past issues. When you observe, you will notice that there are certain times when the visitation occurs of a generational iniquity. As with my son, it occurred whenever we got into an argument. As for Nick and Ester's story, it occurred whenever they went on a trip that involved "venturing out." It can be time related, such a particular time of day or year. If what you are facing involves the visitation of a generational iniquity, the patterns you experience are clues to what and when it occurred in previous generations.

Persistence

A generational iniquity has the characteristic of persistence. Visitations of its influence will continue to occur despite our efforts. They may come and go for a time, but they won't completely go away. Until the source is identified and confessed, the only thing we can do is to resist the influence whenever it happens.

As with my son and me, despite my efforts to do the right thing, the conflict between us kept recurring. Since it persisted, even after dealing with any personal roots from my childhood, this indicated that the source was from somewhere other than my own issues. My efforts to resist the influence, head into the conflict and deal with any fallout were indeed helpful. But this didn't prevent the influence from coming back again. It only provided temporary fixes.

The persistence of generational influences can be wearying as it requires perseverance on our part to resist it. But through persevering, we eventually grow in our character and become more successful in resisting. We will learn that, just because we feel a certain way, that doesn't mean we have to give in. In addition, we will grow in our discernment, acknowledging that not every feeling we have is our own.

Previous Generations

The influence of a generational iniquity visits us, motivating us to react the same way as our ancestors who committed the iniquity. The context in which the influence occurs is a clue to what occurred generationally.

The similarities to what we are experiencing compared to what happened in previous generations are an obvious characteristic of generational iniquity. For example, if you're struggling with finances through no fault of your own, and so did your ancestors, that's a very good indicator that there is a generational iniquity involved. In such cases, you need to consider what family dynamics you have seen or what family stories you have heard. Are there any similarities in your own life to what happened historically? Perhaps all you know is something general about the kind of events that happened to your ancestors, but you have no other details. For instance, you may know that your great grandfather was a criminal, but you don't know what his crimes were. If so, ask the Lord to show you what you need to know.

Concerning my son and me, I was aware of some family stories in which there was animosity between father and son. So, I prayed through these stories first. After doing so, I asked the Lord for any other instances of which I didn't know. He eventually showed me an event in my family's history with the same theme.

The important thing is to pray through what you do know, and ask the Lord to reveal what you don't know. Then, commit everything to Him in prayer.

Things to Consider

- After reading this chapter and looking back on your life, can you think of times when you might have been struggling with feelings and thoughts that may not have been only your own?
- In what ways did this experience fit (or not fit) the characteristics of the influence of a generational iniquity? Has this been an on-going pattern? If so, how?
- What type of issues have you encountered that, despite your efforts, continued to persist?
- What character qualities has God been developing in your life during your times of resistance?
- What are some family stories you have heard that are similar to what you have experienced in your own life?

Dealing with Generational Iniquity

If they confess their iniquity
and the iniquity of their forefathers...
Leviticus 26:40

They Will Never Understand

n Japan, I experienced some challenges while speaking at some conferences. For one, I had to use a translator. Since he was translating, he had to speak half of the time. This meant that I had to condense my one-hour talk to half an hour. In addition, I had to be careful to speak in short, concise sentences, which disrupted my normal flow of speaking. I also soon learned that there were certain words, phrases and jokes that don't translate well or aren't understood. Whenever this occurred, my translator would have to stop in the middle of my talk and ask me for clarity. This was reasonable, though distracting. As a result, I became more watchful about my words and phrases. I soon found myself doubting if my audience was even going to understand my talk.

While these difficulties are fairly normal when using a translator, this particular experience had an added dimension to it. Usually, I'm able to sense and read my audience, which assists me in connecting with them. But for some reason, I wasn't able to do so this time, which only added to the oddness of my experience.

While simultaneously speaking and having to manage all of these little frustrations, the thought, "Do they understand me?" kept plaguing me. It was like an annoying fly that kept buzzing in my ear and wouldn't go away. This only made matters worse. I found myself wrestling with my confidence as a teacher, doubting my ability to help the audience understand. At times, I stumbled over my words and had to stop to find my place in the talk again. Yet, I continued on, despite the distractions. I found that to do so was taking a lot of extra energy to resist and persist. Though the talk went well, it was more challenging and took much more effort than normal. This occurred every time I spoke through out the week.

The last day ended with a time spent in worship and gratitude to God. During this time, a strong feeling of grief came over me. As I pondered it, I sensed it was something generational. Listening with my spirit, I heard these words: "They will not understand." Immediately, I could feel my spirit begin to grieve over this statement.

I asked the Lord for clarity. What He showed me was that my spirit was grieving over something an ancestor of mine had done. My ancestor had judged the Asian people for being different, rather than identifying with what they had in common. This resulted in him choosing to disconnect from them. In addition, he minimized any responsibility he had to pray for, care for or help them if needed. He did this by deciding, "Oh, they won't understand (because they are so different). They eat strange foods. They talk funny. They have strange customs."

As I heard this, I began to cry, knowing what an awful thing it is for one to make judgments toward people from another nation. So in prayer, I repented for what my ancestor had done.

Seventeen months later, I got to return to Japan to speak again, and something astonishing happened. This time my experience was so different! I was able to connect with my audience. I could easily interact with them, and I was so much more at ease around them. My interpreter even noticed, remarking to me more than once how different I was from the last time. A Japanese pastor said the same. Most importantly, I could sense that the audience understood what I was teaching. And even if there were some who didn't, they never became a distraction to me.

It took a lot of effort to resist and to wrestle against the distraction of: "They won't understand." But once it was removed, all of that energy it took to resist became available to pour into my speaking and interactions with the audience. It took going to Japan for this generational iniquity to visit me. It took an understanding of generational iniquity and inquiring of the Lord to recognize and identify it. And after praying through the iniquity, it took returning to Japan to experience the good fruit, confirming that it had been removed.

The following is a helpful acrostic to remember when addressing a possible generational iniquity (RIPE):

Recognize the influence of a generational iniquity,

Identify the source,

Pray through it, and...

Experience the removal of a generational iniquity's influence.

Recognition
Recognizing the influence of a generational iniquity is the first step. This allows us to be aware of its ability to influence, and to look out for it. If what we are experiencing has the characteristics mentioned in the previous chapter, it's a good indication that there is a generational iniquity involved.

If I hadn't known about the influence of generational iniquities, I might have ignored the sadness I had felt at the conference in Japan. Or, I may have taken it on and attributed it to something in myself. But knowing about the influence of generational iniquities, this enabled me to consider it as a possible reason for my experience.

A generational iniquity can be influencing us without us even knowing it. We may have grown so accustomed to its influence that we don't question it. We may have adopted subtle ways of thinking and perceiving that aren't entirely correct. These shifts in our outlook are often unconscious attempts to make life more tolerable. What it means to be a man or a woman, takes on a different meaning. Even one's perception of who God is may be affected. Such shifts may color how we perceive subjects such as marriage, sex, love, money, success, etc. Yet these ways of thinking may not have been ours in the first place. We may have just inherited them from our ancestors. Just knowing that this is possible allows us to recognize the possible influence of a generational iniquity.

This is why God's Word is so important. It allows us to compare our various beliefs, feelings and perceptions against what the Lord says in Scripture. When our perceptions don't line up with God's Word, it is we who must be called into question, not God's Word. Thus, God's Word helps us to recognize false perceptions we may have. This helps us to consider whether we may be under the influence of a generational iniquity or not.

Identify

The next step is to identify the source of the generational iniquity. This may take some time. There are several things you can do to accomplish this:

- Recall any family stories you already know.
- Go ask someone who may know your family history.
- Research your family history.
- Ask the Lord to reveal to you what you don't know about your family history.

Some of us already know, or have heard, certain family stories. If so, consider the similarities between some of the stories and what you are experiencing. For instance, if there are patterns of mistrust in your life, do any of the family stories reflect this theme? If you have struggled with insecurity, did any of your parents or grandparents do so as well? If so, what happened to cause this to happen? What is the story?

Also, consider what isn't being told. My father never said he resented his father, and yet, I know of stories of when they didn't get along. Though my father didn't speak badly of his father, he rarely, if ever, spoke of him at all. However, he spoke freely of his mother. This appeared that he did not have

81

much good to say about his father, indicating possible resentment.

Because my son and I struggled with animosity, it is easy to assume my father did with his father. So, I have confessed any animosity my father may have had toward his father.

I remember one of the few stories my father used to tell. His father had made him a promise but didn't keep it. At the end of the story, my father would then say that it didn't matter because he took care of himself. As I considered this story, it was as if he resented his father, holding animosity towards him. Whether he actually did or not, I confessed it anyway so as to deal with any resent he may have had.

Another resource for family stories is other relatives or family members. Ask them questions. They often know things and have had experiences you have not had. In some instances, you can do research about your family history. Perhaps there are books available. If so, you take what you do know and see if you can find more information.

One thing I would encourage you to do is to ask the Lord to show you what happened in the family history. This is especially helpful when we don't know your family history, or no one wants to tell us.

When asking the Lord about historical events, what I typically ask are questions like: "Who else in the family line experienced something similar to me?," "When else in the family line did this occur?" or, "What happened, historically, in our family that was very similar?" Keep in mind that it isn't important how long ago such events occurred. Knowing specific dates won't undo the generational iniquity. Knowing what the iniquities were and the negative decisions made, this is what's important. The objective is to identify any possible hidden historical events that are similar to what we are experiencing. Then pray, confessing the iniquities.

When it comes to generational iniquities, there are basically three components that we are trying to identify:

The Events - What events occurred historically? What are the stories?

The Iniquities - What specific iniquities occurred? For example: resentment, lying, deception, quitting, murder, turning away from God, etc.

The Decisions – When these events took place, what negative decisions were made by our ancestors? What lies did they choose to believe?

Once we have identified the source of a generational iniquity, we can offer it in prayer of confession to the Lord. We have the authority, as descendants and representatives of our ancestors, to confess generational iniquities so as to put an end to their influence.

Here's how to pray:

Tell what happened by sharing the details of what you know, what was revealed and who was involved. Start with the stories you already know, and then include any the Lord has shown you.

Confess the sinful responses committed by your ancestors.

Renounce any lies they believed and any wrong decisions they made.

Give thanks for any good things your ancestors have done, and the good attributes God created in them, despite what they did wrong.

If it was revealed that someone had sinned against your ancestors, it is important, as a representative of your family line, to forgive such individuals.

Experience Change

The natural by-product of confessing a generational iniquity is change. If we pray through something and nothing changes, it is better to have done so than not at all. Also, keep in mind that sometimes change doesn't occur right away. Give it some time.

Often, the most noticeable change is that it becomes easier to break bad habits. Old ways of thinking either disappear or become easier to resist. Changes in our circumstances and experiences may even occur. Either way, any changes will come about naturally because the influence is gone.

Other Sources of Iniquity

Though we inherit iniquities through our family line, we also inherit in other ways. These can be such as things nationality, positions, roles and ownership. Whenever we are granted something or given stewardship over something, we get all that comes with it. What some of us may not realize is that we also inherit any iniquities the previous person may have committed, even if they were not our ancestor.

For instance, if you are given a certain job position, you inherit all the accomplishments of the previous person who held the same position. You don't have to redo all of the work they did to gain the benefits. Rather, you get to build upon what they did. However, you also inherit any of the negative things (iniquities) they may have done, which will make your job harder unless you undo them.

This principle concerning inheritance is true of our nationality and leadership positions we are given, and even any homes, possessions, and land that become ours. This will covered more specially in other chapters.

Things to Consider

- Are there any family stories that reveal issues that are similar to ones you continue to experience? If so, what are they?
- Who could you ask about your family history? Make a list of questions you would like to ask them.
- What are some other sources where you might be able to get information about your family history?
- Before you pray through a generational iniquity, be sure to identify and write down, at least, the following:
  - What was the historical event?
  - What was the sinful response resulting in an iniquity?
  - What decisions were made as a result?
- With a friend, pray through the information you have gathered.

Inherited by Tradition

See to it that no one takes you captive through
philosophy and empty deception,
according to the tradition of men,
according to the elementary principles of the world,
rather than according to Christ.
Colossians 2:8

The Children are Obligated

hen Nancy's husband was hospitalized, she naturally had to take on more responsibilities, seeing to all that needed to be done at home and with their business. During this trying time, she was pregnant. To her credit, she was able to rise to the occasion, but the stress and exhaustion eventually overwhelmed her. The most frustrating thing for Nancy was that she was so tired all of the time, not being able to get enough sleep. And, with the sleepless nights adding up, things were getting worse. Nancy tried all sorts of remedies in an attempt to stop the insomnia. She went to doctors for medication, naturopaths for natural solutions and friends for prayer. At times, some of these helped, but they were short-lived. Her situation was getting hopeless.

As Nancy shared all that she was going through, it became apparent that, in the midst of her being responsible, she'd also taken on the burden of others' emotions. She felt obligated to somehow "fix" them. As a child, she had felt obligated in a similar way toward her parents, and she had never questioned it. It was like this was her job in life. Now, it had become accentuated to the point that she could no longer keep it up.

With this theme in mind, Nancy made a list of all the times she had taken on responsibility for the emotions of others. She had done this not only with her parents but also with her husband. So she prayed through her list, giving up responsibility for the emotions emotions of others. She also renounced the many decisions she had made, such as: "I can't disappoint others," "I'm responsible for other people's feelings," "I'm responsible to bring relief to others' anxiety," and more.

As Nancy dealt with the root causes from her childhood up to the present day, the Lord revealed that there was a generational cause as well. There was demonic influence in her family line that was attempting to perpetuate the lies that Nancy had believed. It was the practice in her ancestral culture to dedicate the children at the religious temple, for the purpose of protection and blessing in life. This is where the demonic influence was first given access.

Desiring blessing and protection for one's children is a wonderful thing. However, even out of ignorance, dedicating one's children to a god other than the Lord brings about bondage. It turned out that several demons had been attached to Nancy's family line, since they had been given permission through her ancestors. Because each previous generation was under this same bondage, their attempt to "bless" their children was really out of their need to be rescued from the bondage they too were under. This put the children in an unspoken obligation to be responsible their parents' troubles, which was only reinforced through daily family dynamics.

Nancy's grandfather had played a huge role in reinforcing many of these dynamics. One of the ways he did this was to make everyone feel defeated, especially the women. This was an attempt to control them. This oppression of women was another part of Nancy's culture, of which her grandfather took advantage. He used the traditions and culture to justify what he did. Because it was part of their culture, no one questioned his actions. Many, especially the women, felt obligated to comply.

In prayer, Nancy honored her ancestors by thanking God for their desire to bless their children. But then she went on to confess the iniquities of doing so through wrong ways. She renounced all obligations to the family temple and its gods, as well as all of the cultural practices and beliefs that weren't in

87

keeping with God's Word. She also prayed through the many iniquities her grandfather had committed.

As a result, the darkness lifted off of her. This freed Nancy's heart and mind so she could more clearly see the ways she had been mistreated. She no longer saw it as acceptable. This allowed her to avoid getting trapped in old ways of thinking and emotional manipulations of others. With this new freedom, for several weeks Nancy spent time each day praying through various layers of similar generational iniquities as she asked the Lord for more insight. This was especially necessary, since it was something that had been reinforced for many generations.

As a result of all of her hard work, Nancy now feels stronger, able to resist the cultural values of her parents which are not in line with God's Word. She found this especially true whenever her parents would try to obligate her to "fix" them. She is now able to distinguish what her role is when helping others, which is to do so without taking emotional responsibility for them. She feels no longer obligated. The confusion no longer comes over her. And, she is now able to sleep!

We inherit many wonderful things through our culture. But we can also inherit the influence of generational iniquities through the traditions of our families and our cultural. As a matter of fact, some cultural values may be rooted in generational iniquities.

I remember a story about a family who had a tradition in the way they cooked a roast. While the mother was preparing a roast, the daughter asked her a question. She had seen her mother prepare the roast on many occasions, but something caught her attention that day. As her mother would always do, she cut off both ends of the roast before placing it in a pan and putting the pan into the oven. So the little girl asked, "Why do you always cut off both ends of the roast?" Her mother's reply was, "Well, that's how my mother taught me."

Later on, the mother began to think to herself, "Why *do* we always cut off both ends of the roast?" She had never thought to ask why. So she went and asked her mother, "Why did you always cut off both ends of the roast before putting it into the pan to cook?" Her mother's reply was, "That's what your grandmother taught me." But this didn't answer her question: what purpose did this serve? Up until then, each generation had just assumed that there was a good reason, simply because it was the way they had always done it. No one questioned it.

So since great-grandmother was still alive, she was asked the same question: "Why do we always cut off both ends of the roast before placing it in a pan to cook?" Holding her hands in front of her, several inches apart, great-grandmother replied, "Well, I only had a pan that was this big." The only reason she did it was so the roast would fit in the pan!

This illustrates how we often approach traditions. We do certain things but have no idea why, yet no one thinks to question them. It is not to question out of rebellion. Rather, it is to get clarity, get understanding and recall purpose. For a tradition without meaning is empty, and a tradition for tradition's sake is bondage. Traditions aren't meant to be served, but rather to give meaning and richness to our lives. "That's just the way we do it" is not adequate. If a tradition has lost its meaning, its meaning needs to be recovered; otherwise there is no reason to it. And if its meaning can't be found, it should be removed, or at least replace the tradition with one that is meaningful.

The purpose of a tradition is to remind us of who we are, where we come from, what we have overcome and where we are going. It tells us about life, our history and God. So, when we practice a certain tradition, we immediately remember such things. And when we are asked why we maintain a certain tradition, we provide a rich and wonderful reason that is inviting, encouraging and meaningful.

Most family traits, practices and traditions are wonderful. They bring meaning to our uniqueness. They reinforce our good roots, our history and what special traits God has placed in us as a culture, people group or family. These give us a sense of meaning and purpose.

The traditions the Lord gave were for this very purpose. All of the things He instructed His people to do were for their remembrance of all of the wonderful things He had done, and so their children would put their trust in God (Joshua 4:6-7, 21-24). They done with the anticipation that their children would ask, "Why do we do this?" And then the parents would have an answer, replying about all God had done and how wonderful He is and that how great His promises are. And therefore, their children could know that they too can put their trust in the Lord!

The Lord did not prohibit us from having our own traditions, such as commemorations, celebrations, seasonal dinners, festivals, etc. These are important too. But they are not healthy if they are not in keeping with God's Word.

Yet, how often have we heard it said, "That's just part of their culture" with no explanation? Or, "That's just how [insert name of people group] are" as if what they do is normal. Perhaps we have said to ourselves, "Oh, that's just the way we do thing," "That's how we were raised," or, "It's our tradition." Without thinking, we somehow turn something into a non-moral issue if it is attributed to culture or tradition. But this is a deception.

We tend to have the same attitude toward defects in our personal character, saying things like, "This is just the way I am. My father was given to anger, and my grandfather was too. It's just part of my heritage." It is as if uncontrolled anger, pride, depression, stoic-ness, passivity or any other negative and sinful characteristics become "normal" just because we attribute them to our ancestors. In so doing, we allow such traits to become a way of life, and to control our thinking. Thus, we end up reinforcing and justifying a generational iniquity.

But simply because we label a trait or practice as "culturally normal" or as "a tradition", this doesn't make it okay. Without even realizing it, what we're really saying is that culture and tradition are morally neutral. But they are not. So on one hand, we need to honor those wonderful aspects of our culture, while taking into consideration those that are rooted in generational iniquities.

God has put many unique features into each culture. One culture in itself isn't necessarily better than another. The specialness of each nationality is important to God. Each nation and people group has unique purposes, as well as talents, dress, music, worship, dance, perspectives, celebrations and more. These things, in themselves, are morally neutral. It is their expression and practice which may or may not be.

For instance, in one particular culture, when a child is born, it is tradition for the mother to visit the witchdoctor. The witchdoctor then "blesses" the child with good health by putting a mixture of cow manure on the child's freshly cut umbilical cord. Because there is such a high infant mortality rate, many mothers fear that if they don't do this, chances are high that their children will die, when in fact, it is this very tradition that has caused many infant deaths. However, a mother in this culture would be considered neglectful if she didn't do this practice. As result of this tradition, they are in bondage.

The tradition of wanting to bless a child upon its birth is wonderful and is found in almost all cultures. Yet in the previous example, the means of accomplishing this is terrible. It's based upon fear and superstition, creating an ongoing cycle of high infant mortality for subsequent generations.

Every culture is from an original family that, over many years, grew larger and larger. Eventually, it became a nation, developing its own unique culture and traditions. Therefore, one's culture is, essentially, the result of various passed-on family dynamics and values (good and bad). One's traditions are an outgrowth of these values. Many of these traditions are good and meaningful, stemming from positive historical events. But those originating from generational iniquities were founded upon historical events as well. And, as generations come and go, the details about the original events are often lost. As a result, all that is left are the traditions themselves.

91

And, if keeping these traditions becomes more important than loving and caring for people, this a good indication that a generational iniquity at the foundation of the tradition. Jesus experienced this as well (Matthew 15).

In my own culture concerning men, I've often heard it said, "That is just the way men are. Boys will be boys." But where in the Bible does it say that it is okay for men behave sinfully? When is sin ever excusable, no matter what age or gender?

Unfortunately, many people, Christian or not, have accepted such thinking without questioning it. I've heard it said by others that, "It's only normal for teens to rebel." Normal? Why is rebellion normal? Rebellion is sin. So when did it suddenly become okay when one is a teen?

Rather than addressing what tempts teens to rebel and helping them, it is minimized and excused. While it might be normal for teens to be tempted to rebel, it's neither acceptable nor allowable behavior.

I've also heard it said that, "Women are just emotional." Isn't this really said so men can excuse themselves from listening to what women have to say when they're emotional? Where does it say in Scripture that we can ignore women when they're like this? However, at the same time, this doesn't excuse a woman's behaviors just because she sometimes experiences more emotions than a man.

These and other such cultural statements are often attempts to explain away or excuse another's behavior. In reality, we are lowering the way things ought to be, as God designed them. This is often done so we don't have to take responsibility for our weaknesses, inadequacies and inabilities. Rather than meet the challenge, we make things more acceptable and tolerable for ourselves. When we look closer at inappropriate and questionable cultural traditions, we often find this at the heart of them. The origins of such traditions are often found in historical iniquities that have been forgotten but, nonetheless, perpetuated throughout the generations.

Jesus confronted several cultural traditions that existed during the time He was on earth. These are referred to as the "traditions of men" (Colossians 2:8). On one occasion, Jesus healed on the Sabbath. In doing so, He violated the religious rules of that time, which were part of the culture, but they weren't God's rules. For the religious, it had become more important to follow the traditions than to show mercy. How did this possibly happen? Showing mercy can often be inconvenient and humbling. One might have to deal with people who are difficult and unkempt. One may have to go out of their way. Being merciful may cost time, energy and other personal sacrifices. Perhaps doing such things was beneath the religious leaders of Jesus' time. But what better way than a tradition so as to avoid (or excuse) being soiled or distracted from religious duties.

Another time, Jesus publicly refuted the cultural rule: children aren't to bother a teacher. The rule was, essentially, "Children are neither to be seen nor heard" – sound familiar? When the disciples tried to shoo away the children, Jesus rebuked them (Matthew 19:14). He then invited the children to come to Him so He might pray for them. Here we see that, at times, not all aspects of culture, even the one in which Jesus grew up, are right. Yet at the same time, Jesus honored many of the other customs and traditions of the culture in which He lived, as long as they did not violate God's Word.

So how do we know when a tradition is wrong? The answer is: whenever it violates God's Word. We see this in another example by Jesus. Once, Jesus' disciples didn't wash their hands before eating, thus they were accused of not keeping the "tradition of the elders" (Matthew 15:2). Jesus then confronted the accusers, pointing out how they violated the commandments of God for the sake of their tradition (Mark 7:8).

Jesus doesn't condemn culture. But He also doesn't honor those traditions that aren't in keeping with God's Word.

Often, it is difficult for us to become free of a cultural tradition that is based upon a generational iniquity, especially when there are several factors reinforcing it. For one, we have lived the majority of our lives under such traditions. As a result, we have formed habits and regular practices around them. In addition, we have family members, friends and events that continue to reinforce them. Lastly, there are the many previous generations that have reinforced these traditions. But, by being diligent to identify and pray through various generational iniquities, we can begin to remove their influences. Just like Nancy did.

God doesn't want us to get rid of our culture. He wants to redeem our culture. In many cases, various negative aspects have gotten mixed into one's culture over the years. So we need to filter out and deal with those that aren't good while preserving those that are.

Addressing Inappropriate Family Cultural or Traditions
- Recognize the negative patterns in your life and your family that appear to be related to your family's cultural or traditions and aren't in keeping with God's word.
- Ask the Lord to show you what occurred historically that started these inappropriate traditions.
- In prayer to the Lord:
  - Share the historical events that created these inappropriate traditions.
  - Confess the iniquities committed that established them.
  - Renounce any wrong beliefs held by your family.
  - Honor your ancestors by thanking God for good things they did, including the ways they meant well while confessing their wrong applications.
  - Thank God for your culture and its desirable aspects.
- Ask the Lord to show you what His redemptive purposes are for such cultural practices. In other words, what are the right applications for the traditions that your ancestors applied wrongly? If appropriate, put these right applications into practice.

Things to Consider

- What are some family traits about which you have found yourself saying, "That's just the way we are in our family"?
- What are some cultural norms that people rarely or never question, but are really not based upon God's word?
- What are some of the wonderful traditions and dynamics of your culture and family history?
- What are some of the spoken and unspoken traditions, rules and norms in your family and/or culture that are contradictory to God's Word? Make a list.
- What events do you remember and what family stories have you heard that reinforce and illustrate the practices of these traditions?
- If you have identified a family or cultural tradition that is possibly connected to a generational iniquity, go through the steps shown under the heading, "Addressing Family Cultural Traditions."

Inherited by Position

Now there was a famine in the days of David
for three years, year after year;
and David sought the presence of the LORD.
And the LORD said, "It is for Saul and his bloody house,
because he put the Gibeonites to death."
II Samuel 21:1

A Spirit of Competition

While teaching at a seminar in Japan, I had a meal with some of the other teachers. During the meal, people began sharing some amazing things they had seen the Lord do in the recent past. Initially, this was a good experience, as it was exciting to hear stories about what the Lord had done. But then a subtle change began to take place. I could feel a temptation coming over the group, tempting us to outdo one another in telling stories. At the same time, I sensed that a demon was present. Specifically, it was trying to influence me and another person, the only two Americans at the table. So as not to alarm anyone, I silently rebuked the demon, and the temptation to compete lifted off.

Later, when I was by myself, I asked the Lord why the demon was there in the first place, and why it seemed to have so much influence. He showed me that there was a reason it was specifically attacking the two Americans and not the others. When some Americans came to Japan many years ago, they had committed a historical iniquity. The demon was taking advantage of this legal ground to influence. When some churches from America brought the message of the Gospel to this region in Japan, they also brought an attitude of competiveness. Thus, they defiled the Japanese churches in the area with their own iniquities.

There were two different groups who started churches among the Japanese in the area. But instead of being united and joining their resources, they became competitive in their hearts toward one another, competing for members to join their church. In addition, there were some who took advantage of the Japanese way of hospitality. Instead of seeking to serve, they sought to be served by the Japanese people.

The attack by the demon now made sense. Since I am American, as well as a member of the body of Christ, I was a representative of those who had committed the historical iniquities, despite that neither my ancestors nor I had committed such iniquities. This is why the demon attacked the other American teacher as well. So in prayer, I confessed the iniquities of those who had come to Japan and had sinned against the Japanese people.

Later, I shared this experience with one of the Japanese pastors. He confirmed that there has been strong competitiveness among churches in Japan. In part, this came from the competitive Japanese business practices, which had transferred over to the Japanese church. But those who came from America had contributed their part, which reinforced the problem.

The next day, prior to my talk, I shared what the Lord had shown me with those attending the seminar. There were many pastors and their wives present. As I shared, something unexpected happened: I began to weep. I could feel, in my heart, the great sadness of what had been done by those who historically. My spirit was grieving. I then asked the Japanese audience for forgiveness for what we, the American Christians, had done, thus owning our part. They forgave.

As a result, many were touched. There were those who cried. One woman shared how much this gesture blessed her. In addition, the demon has never returned to attack us again.

Whenever we are given a position, we inherit not only the responsibilities, benefits and rewards of that position, we also inherit any historical iniquities committed by those who previously held the position. In addition, our attitudes and actions, while in the position, will leave behind an influence (good and bad) for those who inherit our position. What is more significant isn't so much what we accomplish. Rather, it is the character we produce and maintain while in a position. This is what we leave behind.

Throughout your life, you take on various roles and positions – sometimes more than one at a time. Just to name a few examples: son/daughter, parent, employee, boss, church member, citizen of a town or nation, etc. It makes no difference whether you are a maid versus an owner of a big hotel, or a janitor versus a professor at a university. In whatever positions you hold, you inherit and leave behind an influence. This is also true of any group structure, such as a nation, an organization, a city, or even a church. It is true of partnerships, such as in a marriage or a business. Your marriage and your children will be influenced by the generational blessings and iniquities, of yours and your wife's family lines. Any business co-ownership will be influenced by the combined inherited influences of the two owners. Any organization will be so by the combined influences of the leaders. The influence is from the top down, affecting all those under their authority.

Years ago, while I was working at a particular business, another manager left. Seeing a need that I thought I could fulfill, I took on one of his previous responsibilities. But when I did, negative things began to happen. Without knowing why, I began to feel oppressed. While at work, I found myself getting overly angry. I found myself tempted to manipulate in order to get things done. None of these were things with which I normally struggle. I finally noticed that this all began when I took on the new responsibility.

So I asked the Lord why I was experiencing this oppression. He showed me that the previous manager had a problem with anger and would often give in to expressing it behind closed doors. In addition, he had often made decisions out of anger. I found out from others that this was true, and that he had also coerced various venders in order to get a good deal or to make things happen. Even though the previous manager was gone, I inherited the defilement of his iniquity because I had taken on some of the responsibilities of his position. I was tempted to react like his iniquities for they were influencing me.

So I confessed, in prayer to the Lord the iniquities of the previous manager. The result: the oppression of the anger left, and I was no longer tempted to manipulate in order to get things done.

This same phenomenon happened to David when he succeeded Saul as king. A famine had been going on for several years (II Samuel 21:1). When he asked the Lord why, the Lord told him that it was because of something Saul had done while he was the king. Saul had broken a treaty, which had been made many generations before, between Israel and the Gibeonites. Upon learning this, David, as king, made restitution for what Saul had done. And, as a result, the land was restored (II Samuel 21:14).

On the flipside, a positive deposit can be left behind as well. At one particular job I had, there was a lot of oppression that came with the position. I had to resist being passive, while at the same time confronting issues and maintaining respectfulness towards those in authority. Years later, after I had left this job, the person who had taken my position told me how much of a difference I had made. She could actually feel the difference. She said it was like I had cleared a path for her, making her job much easier to undertake. Though there were still challenges which she had to wrestle, my efforts in prayer and in sowing good character had made things less difficult for her.

Identifying an Iniquity Inherited by Position

Recognize the Iniquity – In the position you are holding, what is the theme of the oppression you are experiencing? Like a generational iniquity, what characteristics does it have that indicate that it might be an iniquity inherited by position?

Examine Yourself and Repent as Needed – It's important to be sure that you have repented of ways in which you have sinned in a similar manner. This needs to be done before proceeding any further. Otherwise, you'll be hindered from discovering and removing any historical defilement, since you may be contributing to it. So ask the Lord to show you ways in which you have sinned similarly. Then, be sure to confess what He shows you, and do the opposite by doing good.

Uncover Any Historical Iniquities – What historical iniquities were committed by those who once held the position? In many cases, you may already know. Perhaps you witnessed some of these events or have heard stories. You can also do a little research by asking others. In addition, be sure to ask the Lord to show you what may have happened. You need to uncover what sinful historical actions and decisions were made by person(s) who previously held the position.

Pray through the Iniquities Inherited by Position

- Share the historical events by telling what had happened.
- Confess the iniquities committed.
- Confess any negative decisions and/or curses made by the previous person(s) in the position.
- Ask the Lord to bless the position and to grant the wisdom to carry out its responsibilities.
- If needed, seek restitution for those who may have been hurt by the person who had been in the position previously.
- Do good things in the position you are in so as to leave a blessing for whoever may inherit your position. This will also bless whoever is over you as well as those under your position.

Things to Consider

- What are some positions you hold, or have held, in which you realize you may have inherited the influence of an iniquity? What makes you think so?

- Looking back, can you see a connection between when you took on a certain position or task and when specific difficulties began? What was the theme of the ongoing difficulties?

- Gather any information concerning any iniquities committed by those who held the position previously.

- Ask the Lord to show you what events transpired prior to you taking the position, which may have caused the trouble.

- If you've identified an iniquity inherited by position, go through the steps shown previously under the heading, "Praying Through an Iniquity Inherited by Position."

- What are some things you can do to make the position easier for the person who will someday inherit it?

- Can you think of positions you have taken on where it seemed like someone had made a much clearer path for you? If so, take time to thank the Lord for the person who had the position prior to you, asking the Lord to bless the individual. If that person is still alive, let him or her know how much you appreciate them.

- Looking back, were there any positions that you held where you may had left defilement? If so, confess it to the Lord as sin and ask the Lord to bless whoever inherited your position. If needed, seek to make restitution.

Inherited by Ownership

For the land has become defiled,
therefore I have brought its punishment upon it,
so the land has spewed out its inhabitants.
Leviticus 18:25

And I sought for a man among them,
that should make up the hedge,
and stand in the gap before me for the land...
Ezekiel 22:30

Unable to Rest

Looking back, Jim and Linda realized that many of their difficulties started soon after they purchased a particular piece of land. While living on the property, Linda had four severe miscarriages. Even though she eventually gave birth to one child, it was a difficult pregnancy. During most of the pregnancy, Linda's heart would beat unceasingly fast, which was very stressful for her. These were just a few of the many difficulties that occurred. Even after they had sold the land, Linda had times when she felt troubled whenever she thought about that the land. It was as if it haunted her.

As Linda pondered the possible connection between the difficulties and the time when they lived on that property, the Lord showed her something. He reminded her of a woman who had been employed in their business. Linda had never trusted this woman, not knowing why at first. Linda sensed that there was some connection between this woman and the land.

While listening to the Lord, He revealed that the woman Linda distrusted had been practicing witchcraft behind the scenes and had done so against Linda's family. There was also a historical event of iniquity had taken place on the land. The woman through witchcraft had taken advantage of this historical iniquity as an access point to curse Jim and Linda. They were vulnerable only because they had become the new owners of the land, and therefore, they got all that came with the land, even the historical iniquities.

So we asked the Lord to show us what had happened historically. He revealed that, many years ago, there were native people who had lived peacefully on the land. But one day, that all changed, as many became sick and died. A particular elder grew bitter as he watched those he loved suffer in sickness and then die while he could do nothing about it. He noticed that this all seemed to begin when non-natives moved into the area. So he began to blame them for what had happened. He also resented them for how they had disrespected the land. When they harvested trees and built roads, instead of being good managers of the land, they were harsh and destructive, having no regard for the environmental impact.

The elder eventually became so bitter that he cursed the non-natives. His curses included: "May you suffer great loss and pain," "May you bear the iniquity of the land," "May these same atrocities (such as loss of family members) come upon you," and, "May you not rest until you have paid for all you have done." As a former steward of the land, he left a defilement of bitterness and curses on the land, which would affect any future owners.

Keep in mind that the curses of the elder could only affect the non-natives if they had indeed committed sin; for it is unconfessed sin that gives curses access to afflict. "Like a sparrow in its flitting, like a swallow in its flying, So a curse without cause does not alight" (Proverbs 26:2). The curses had access to the non-natives because they had sinned and were not repentant. As a result, any future owners of the property became subject to the curses.

In prayer, as a previous owner of the land, Linda acknowledged the bitterness and curses of the elder. She also confessed the disrespect that the non-natives had shown for the land. She forgave the elder and the people who had disrespected the land. She also forgave the woman who cursed her and her husband as the once owners of the land. Lastly, she blessed the land, and she blessed the present owners who had become the new stewards of the land.

After this, a tremendous relief came over Linda. She no longer felt haunted. In her spirit, she knew that the land was free of the defilement. It brought a peace to her heart, and now she could rest. She no longer feels troubled when she thinks about the land.

I have a 1913 upright piano that was given to me for free. Since the previous owner didn't want it anymore, all I had to do was come and get it. When I got it home and into my garage, I began to smell a repulsive odor. When I investigated, I discovered that a cat had urinated on the piano, which may have been the reason the previous owner was so willing to give it away. Fortunately, I was planning on thoroughly refinishing the piano before bringing it into my house. After much cleaning, stripping, bleaching and sanding every surface of the piano, the odor was gone. And once it was stained and varnished, it became a beautiful piece of furniture, fully restored and with no smell.

In a way similar to my piano with its offensive smell, items we own can also be spiritually defiled. This can happen with any item we acquire. If an item has been involved with an iniquity, it gets associated with that iniquity. The influence of the iniquity remains with the object, and thereafter, it has a spiritual "stench" that affects others whenever they come into contact with it. Therefore, when the item gets transferred to you as a new owner, the defilement of the iniquity comes with it, negatively influencing you, from your behaviors to adversely affecting your welfare, livelihood, health and family. How its defilement tempts you to react, or negatively affects you or your life, this is a clue to how the item was defiled.

Objects are sometimes intentionally defiled. In some instances, the previous owner sinned by placing a curse on it, purposing the object to adversely affect whoever comes into contact with it or takes possession of it. Another way an object can be defiled is when it is used for evil purposes.

Even land can become defiled such as when an iniquity is committed on it. The defilement of the iniquity lingers in the location where it was committed, influencing those who go there but especially the owners This can happen with man-made structures such as houses, offices, buildings, stairwells, hotel rooms and cities. It can also be a landmark, such as a specific street corner, a grove of trees, a place in a forest or even a location at a beach. Here are some verses that refer to the land being defiled: Numbers 35:34, Leviticus 18:25, Jeremiah 3:1, 12:10, and Psalm 106:38.

As for Jim and Linda, by becoming the new owners of the land they purchased, they not only got all the benefits of the land (beauty, seclusion, equity, etc.), they also inherited any iniquities attached to it. But by indentifying those iniquities and confessing them, this removed the defilement, restoring the land.

When some friends of mine moved into a different house, they began to argue more, which was unlike them. It got so bad that they found themselves struggling with thoughts of divorce. Fortunately, they realized that the previous occupants of the house had originally sold it because of divorce. My friends then realized that they, as the new occupants, were being influenced by the iniquities from the previous owners. With this information, they were able to address the situation in prayers of confession, which got rid of the influence.

Those who are more spiritually sensitive understand this ability to sense the defilement of an object or place. Have you ever entered a house and suddenly felt oppressed? Have you ever gone somewhere and felt a darkness or cloud come over you, though you couldn't see it with your physical eyes? Some objects, no matter how innocent in appearance, may have seemed evil or cold when you looked at them, got close to them or even touched them, but you didn't know why. It is likely you were sensing the defilement associated with the object.

When my son was little, we went to a science store. There were all sorts of interesting things to play with. While there, I saw a room that had stars glowing on the ceiling. When I asked my son if he wanted to go in, he said, "No" and turned away with a troubled look. When I asked the Lord why my son had done this, my eyes immediately fell upon a display outside of the door to the room. I saw various books on astrology and similar topics. Though my son was too young to know what these books were about, his spirit knew there was something defiling in the room, and he didn't want to go in.

Once, while I was visiting England, I stayed in a four-story home that was very old. While attempting to go to sleep in the guest room on the third floor, I began to feel tempted by sexual thoughts. Realizing that the enemy was trying to attack me, I prayed for God's help. I also checked to make sure that I hadn't exposed myself to anything that would have made me more vulnerable to temptation. Yet, despite doing all of this, the temptation persisted, which made it impossible for me to sleep. All I could do was to keep praying.

Then the Lord spoke to me, saying, "Ask Me what happened in this room." So I asked, "What happened in this room?" He then revealed to me that, about 60 years earlier, a man had molested a teenage girl in that very room. Since the iniquity had never been confessed, the defilement of it remained, and a demon was attached to it.

In prayer, I exposed the historical event by acknowledging the iniquity that had been committed, and I asked the Lord to cleanse the room. In the name of Jesus, I then commanded the demon of sexual perversion to leave.

After doing this, I was able to rest without having to do ongoing warfare. The influence of the iniquity was gone. The defilement that had been associated with my room had been removed. Now, any future guests wouldn't be affected.

Houses and other such places that are haunted by demons, this happens simply because one or more historical iniquities were committed there. The characteristics of the haunting are almost always in keeping with the original iniquities. As long as these aren't addressed, the haunting will continue. The

106

demon's goal through their haunting is to create fear and to tempt others to sin in a similar manner as the historical iniquities so as to increase the defilement at that location.

I once met a husband and wife whose house was haunted. They often experienced horrible dreams. They shared how, in the middle of the night, they saw what appeared to be a man standing at the foot of their bed. One time, the husband awoke choking, as if someone was trying to kill him. Yet, no real person was there in either case.

The prevailing theme of their haunting was murder. There were demons portraying historic iniquities. So, we asked the Lord for insight. He showed us that the historical iniquities involved hadn't occurred in that house. Rather, there was an iniquity of murder in the family lines of both the husband and the wife. So, in this case, the haunting went with them wherever they moved. As we asked for more insight, the Lord revealed various murders committed by their ancestors. Though the husband and wife were both committed Christians and had never committed murder themselves, this generational influence was plaguing their home.

We first prayed through the historical iniquities of the husband's ancestors. Then, we did the same for the wife. Lastly, we asked the Lord to cleanse and bless their home.

A peace came over the home, and the visitations of the man in the night ceased. So did the bad dreams. The husband felt very much relieved. For many years prior, there were times when he would struggle with thoughts of murder, but he never knew why. Though he never acted on them, they never completely went away. Yet, now, they were gone. As a bonus, their older daughter gave her life to Jesus shortly thereafter.

If you are a tenant or guest of a house, apartment, office or dorm room, as a renter, you have been granted the right to occupy the space and, therefore, you can pray through any iniquities that might be there. This is true of hotel rooms, campsites and public property. Whenever I rent a hotel room, I pray not only for the cleansing of any iniquities, but I also pray a blessing upon the room, which extends to any future occupants.

107

When you take ownership of something, you have the privilege of blessing and committing it for God's purposes and glory. I encourage you to do this for all that you own. I frequently bless my home, inviting God's presence. A friend of mine goes to a church where once a year a leader from his church comes to his home and prays over all the rooms, praying God's blessing. This is done for all the members of his church. What a wonderful thing!

More about Defiled Objects

When items are used for iniquity, they become defiled. This is one of the reasons God often had the Israelites destroy the possessions of the people they conquered (Numbers 33:52; Deuteronomy 12:2-3).

Any and all items used for occult activities are defiled. This includes objects used for, or dedicated in, a ceremony or ritual, or those used to obtain information from a demon or a supposed god. Additional practices include witchcraft, astrology, channeling, palm reading, etc. Those who use and do such things are defiled as well (Leviticus 19:31). Some examples of defiled items are tarot cards, Ouija boards, voodoo dolls and crystal balls. But sometimes, defiled items aren't so obvious, such as jewelry, clothes, art work and tools used by someone else in a defiling manner or for an evil purpose.

If any items you possess are in question, ask the Lord if they have been defiled, and He will show you. Consider praying with a friend, asking together.

If you own items that are defiled, it is very important that you pray over them, asking the Lord to remove all defilement from them. If you know the iniquity behind the object or the Lord shows you, confess the iniquity. And then bless the object for the Lord's glory and purposes. Doing so, you purify and redeem such objects for God's use. If you don't, the defilement will remain, affecting all who come in contact with it.

If an object was used in occult practices or worship, it is very important to destroy it. To destroy means to demolish and, thus, render something completely useless, so it can't be used again, even for another purpose. Moses had the golden calf burned, ground into powder and cast into a lake (Exodus 32:20). He did this even though its gold could have been melted down and used for the temple. In Acts, many people, upon becoming Christians, burned defiled objects they owned, even though they could have sold them for a great deal of money (Acts 19:19).

One last thing I would encourage you to do. Whenever you obtain ownership of something - whether purchased, found or given as a gift - pray over it, asking God to bless it for His glory and purposes. This will ensure a blessing for you and your family, as well as for those who one day may become the new owners.

Praying for a Defiled Location

Identify the Defilement – What bad things keep happening that seem to be associated with a particular location? By identifying the theme of the defilement, this will give you a clue of the historical iniquity that took place.

Uncover Historical Events – Sometimes we know what took place historically. But, in many instances, we may need to do a little research, asking others questions about the history of a particular location. More importantly, if no one knows, we can ask God to reveal it to us. Be sure to record any significant sinful events and the negative decisions others may have made. These are what need to be committed in prayers of confession.

Get an Associate – It's best if you include someone who is associated with the land. This would be someone who either owns, rents or occupies the location. It can also be someone who was associated with the iniquities committed on the location, such as a descendant. Such a person can stand in as a representative when praying.

Utilize Team Effort – If the Lord leads you to pray for a defiled location, I encourage you to do so with a team of other Christians. This will help in getting more insight, and you will all share in the blessing of seeing the land healed.

109

<u>Pray through the Historical Iniquities</u>
- Confess the historical iniquities by telling what happened.
- Confess any negative decisions and curses that may have been made.
- If there is any demonic attachment to the land, command it to leave.
- Ask the Lord to bless the location, as well as its occupants and owners. Try to be specific in your blessing. For instance, if there was depression, bless the place with joy. If there was unrest, bless it with peace and rest.

Things to Consider
- What are some items you own that you now think may have a defilement or curse attached to them? What makes you think so?
- What objects do you own that you need to get rid of? Ask the Lord to show you. Dispose of those that were used for occult practices and purposes while praying prayers of confession and dedication to the Lord over those that weren't.
- Take an inventory of all the things you own, including your home, vehicles, properties, vehicles, furniture, jewelry, etc. Spend the time asking God to bless all these things, committing to Him for His glory and purposes.
- Can you think of some places or locations that may be defiled? What makes you think there is defilement there?
- Take an inventory of the places you occupy (house, apartment, office, etc.). Are there any recurring negative experiences associated with any of these places? If so, ask the Lord if there are any historical iniquities associated, and pray through whatever He shows you.

Removing Generational Influences

Then they will rebuild the ancient ruins,
They will raise up the former devastations;
And they will repair the ruined cities,
The desolations of many generations.
Isaiah 61:4

I'm Through Rescuing

A predominant pattern in Jack's life was of people taking advantage of him. He was a hard worker, generous and didn't mind helping others. But he seemed to attract people who tended to take advantage of his generosity. And, no matter how much he tried to help these people, many didn't improve. This left Jack feeling used and discouraged, since his heart was to help others.

Throughout his life, Jack had taken on the role of "rescuer." As a child, he often witnessed unresolved conflicts between his parents. He wanted things to be better between them, and he thought he could somehow help. So, as he made a decision to rescue them. In other words, he would do whatever it took so his father and mother wouldn't argue. However, this didn't keep them from arguing. In addition, as he got older, his decision caused him to unintentionally attract people who needed to be rescued, and in each case, there was little or no change in their lives.

As it turned out, the role of rescuing others was a pattern in Jack's family. Both of his parents had a habit of "picking up the slack" for others. Though they were generous, giving of their time and money to others, people took advantage of them. Thus, they often felt used and unappreciated. Though Jack saw the generosity of his parents as a good thing, there were times he resented it. This was especially true when his parents' time and attention devoted to helping others took priority over his own needs.

So, Jack prayed through the instances in which he took on the inappropriate responsibility to "rescue" his parents and others, releasing the responsibility back to them. He then confessed his resentment toward his parents, for all of the times they gave their attention away at his expense. He confessed the generational iniquity of "rescuing people" that was on both sides of his family. Thus, he renounced the unspoken family motto: "We will pick up the slack."

The next week, Jack's mother called me to share her appreciation for her son getting prayer ministry. And then, for no apparent reason, she shared a recent conversation she had with her mother (Jack's grandmother). Her mother shared that the Holy Spirit had convicted her of how she had abandoned Jack's mother as a child while attempting to rescue other people. So, she asked her daughter for forgiveness. And then, she made a declaration to her daughter, "I'm through rescuing people!" When she said this, Jack's mother realized that she had done the same thing. So, she replied, "So am I!"

Jack's mother went on to say how, that very week, a relative had asked her husband for money. But, this time, her husband did something different. He refused to do so.

When I asked her if she knew what issues her son had prayed through the week before, she said, "No." She had no idea, since her son hadn't told her anything. Her son's confession concerning the generational iniquity of "rescuing people" hadn't only touched his life, but it had begun affecting his family as well. And, this occurred without their awareness of what Jack had done!

Jack's story demonstrates the impact one person can have upon the lives of other family members, just by being faithful to confess identified generational iniquities. Like most of us, there's usually more than one factor contributing to what we are wrestling against. As with Jack, he had his personal experiences as well as the generational iniquities. Both of these were contributing to his struggle, and both required prayer. By addressing the generational iniquity of "rescuing people," Jack set in motion a change that affected his grandmother, his mother, and his father as well. In turn, this would affect his siblings and subsequent generations as well!

Whenever we pray through a generational iniquity, it removes the influence of that iniquity from the lives of those who were under it. In so doing, we and they have one less factor influencing us to respond and to think in inappropriate ways. This is helpful, but it isn't a guarantee of change. There are several reasons for this.

For one, we each have a free will. So, even though the generational influence is lifted, each person must choose to change. Jack's grandmother, when convicted by the Holy Spirit, was willing to be obedient, and so was his mother. Unfortunately, there are those, who, despite the conviction of the Holy Spirit, resist changing their ways.

Removing generational influence only removes that influence. It doesn't break bad habits formed over the years. Each person still has to choose to resist. As with Jack's parents, they were aware of this inappropriate family dynamic and, at times, attempted to resist it. This built strength of character. As a result, once the influence was removed, it became easier to resist. It is easier to break old habits once the generational influence is gone. At the same time, having generational influences isn't an excuse for bad habits. Until they're dealt with, the Lord expects us to persevere, despite the influences.

Another thing to consider is that a person has lived mush of their life under the reinforcing theme of a generational iniquity. Most likely, he or she has added to it by contributing like behaviors and attitudes. So, even with generational iniquity removed through prayer, there will still remain the influence of what they have personally sown. That's why it was so important for Jack to pray through times in his own life as well.

Consider the story, "Animosity between Father and Son." What helped tremendously was my determination not to let the generational influence get any ground in my relationship with my son by resisting. In the meantime, it was important that I persevered in prayer, seeking the Lord for a solution while confronting any sinful areas in my own life. And then, once the Lord revealed the sources of the influence, the generational iniquities were confessed in prayer. In so doing, this freed my son as well.

Also, consider the story, "If You Venture Out, Bad Things Will Happen to You." As a result of the parents praying through the identified generational iniquities, their children were blessed, as well as having experienced firsthand the power of God's deliverance.

So, praying through generational iniquities not only blesses you, but also blesses extended family members and generations to come by lifting the influences off of them as well.

 Things to Consider

- What are some of the negative patterns or issues that exist in your extended family that are unhealthy?
- What are some of the ways these have occurred in your own life?
- What family history do you know that could be contributing to this?
- Ask the Lord to show you any additional details.
- Pray prayers of confession of any identified generational iniquities.

Wrestling

Jacob "wrestled" with the Lord.
Genesis 32:24-30

We Aren't Going to Make It

everal years ago, I went through a challenging financial experience. Just prior, I had a part-time job, which allowed me to earn extra income in addition to my full-time job. Then, one day, I was faced with a dilemma. The management wanted to pursue business opportunities that would require me to compromise my moral convictions. Despite sharing my concern, the management still wanted to go in the direction it was headed. I struggled greatly with this, trying to figure out how I could keep the job without compromising my convictions.

What made this dilemma even more difficult was that I had poured lots time and energy into my part-time job. Therefore, quitting would feel like all of my work was for nothing. In addition, this job allowed me to be very creative and provided all sorts of possible future opportunities. Even more so, it held the potential promise of full-time work and more income than my present job and, therefore, with it came the possibility of quitting my "mundane" present full-time job.

But, no matter how much I tried to rationalize, I didn't have peace. It all really came down to whether I would compromise my convictions or not. So in the end, I decided that I needed to do the right thing and quit my part-time job.

Looking back, I don't regret my decision. But nonetheless, it did cost me. I no longer had the benefit of the extra income and I gave up the opportunity for a possible new career.

Shortly after I made my decision, an irrational fear came over me. It was pervasive, and I couldn't shake it. I began to

115

worry about our finances, even though we were doing fine. Yes, quitting my side job meant not having the extra money, but we could still pay our bills. We had to adjust our budget and realize that certain goals and plans would have to be put off. Yet, no matter how much I reassured myself that our finances were fine, I couldn't shake the feeling, "We aren't going to make it."

I wrestled with this issue for months. I knew the feelings were irrational, but they wouldn't go away. Some days, they would subside, but they were still under the surface. Other days, it would get so bad that my knees literally began to shake. There were times when I broke out in a sweat when the fear would come over me so strongly. I was often tempted to go back to the part-time job in order to appease the fear. Yet, in the midst of all of this, I decided to bear under it, while not drawing attention to myself. And, just as importantly, I wrestled with the Lord in prayer, asking Him for help and deliverance.

After about six months, the Lord finally freed me. He revealed to me three separate historical events I was bearing under with the theme, "We aren't going to make it!" In all three scenarios, the individuals were under great duress, fearing that they weren't going to make it. And, instead of heading into their circumstances, despite their fears, they gave up. In so doing, they left behind the influence of their iniquity.

With this new understanding, I prayed. I acknowledged the stories of each of the three individuals, confessing their iniquities and renouncing their decision that, "We aren't going to make it." And, after I had prayed, the influence left and has never returned, even when we have have had financial issues.

Looking back at this time of wrestling, I have since gained some insights. For one, the Lord had purposely set up my circumstances to initiate the visitation of a generational iniquity. He knew my convictions would allow me to make the right decision. But, He also knew this experience would challenge me to wrestle with the visitation, and with Him, in prayer. He had a purpose for me, but also one beyond me. He desired for the generational iniquity to be removed, not only for my benefit, but also for generations to come.

So, why didn't the Lord reveal the generational iniquity sooner, rather than later? If He had, and I had prayed through it, this would have minimized all of the difficulties I endured while waiting. It would have saved a lot of time.

However, there are several reasons why He doesn't show us right away the source of a generational iniquity. They following are a few of them.

Perseverance

The Lord wants to teach us that we have a choice to resist and that we don't have obey our feelings and impulses. He wants us to learn that, if we endure long enough, we will eventually get results. More importantly, we will learn that we aren't victims of our feelings, heritage and past.

The very reason for a generation iniquity is because there were those who failed to persevere. Therefore, your time of perseverance is a time to resist this family failure and to replace it with resolve and strength.

Character

The Lord wants to build character into our lives and have it passed on to the subsequent generations. If He always removed the influence of the generational iniquity right away, there would be no godly character built into our lives. Thus, there would be none to pass on to subsequent generations. It is like building muscles. Without something to resist, no character can be built. Allowing us to endure against the generational influence for a season builds character, which will be a blessing to pass on to future generations.

In addition, the Lord is preparing you for what He has next for you. Therefore, He uses the time while you endure against a generational iniquity to make you fit for the plans He has for you. So trust Him, endure well, build character and anticipate good things ahead.

Commitment

The Lord wants to know if we are really committed. Bearing under a generational iniquity for a season is an opportunity for this. In reality, *He* knows that we can be committed. More importantly, He wants *us* to know that we can be committed. Commitment doesn't mean that we won't make mistakes or feel like giving up. Rather, it means that we always get back up whenever we fall.

Spiritual Discernment

The Lord allows us to bear under generational influence so we can identify all that needs to be confessed in prayer. Upon going through this process, we gain greater sensitivity to recognize generational influences, rather than becoming desensitized to them. As a result, we grow in our spiritual discernment and can recognize generational iniquities in others in order to help them.

In the chapter titled, "Visiting the Generations," I pointed out how Abraham struggled with passivity, acting out of fear instead of faith. Instead of laying down his own life for his wife, he acted on his fear by allowing her to be put in harm's way in order to save his own life. One generation later, Isaac, Abraham's son, did the same thing. Then, in the very next generation, Jacob, Isaac's son, faced the same fear for his life (Genesis 31-32).

Jacob was about to face his brother, Esau. In the past, Jacob had taken advantage of Esau and used deception to steal his birthright and blessing. Now, understandably, Jacob feared that Esau would want to kill him.

Here is an interesting side note: if Jacob had waited to see how the Lord would fulfill His word concerning him, instead of manipulating, Jacob wouldn't have been in this predicament. Yet, despite what Jacob had done, God used his offense with his brother to provide Jacob the opportunity to later resist the generational iniquity.

Though Jacob was afraid, he acted differently than his forefathers. The first thing Jacob did was to seek the Lord. He acknowledged his fears and his unworthiness of the Lord's mercy. He then asked for help while recalling the promises the Lord had made to him and his forefathers. In contrast, his forefathers had immediately reacted by making decisions based upon their fears, without seeking the Lord first or recalling His promises.

After doing this, Jacob made a plan. He decided to send gifts to Esau before facing him, hoping this would somehow appease him. After that, Jacob planned to send his wives and children. By sending his wives ahead of himself, he was initially acting in the same manner as his forefathers who had been unwilling to sacrifice their lives on behalf of their wives.

But then, Jacob did several other things that neither Abraham nor Isaac had done. He resisted lying. He instructed his servants to tell the truth if they encountered Esau and were asked, "Whose flocks are these?" But, perhaps even more significantly, Jacob rose to the occasion when God challenged him. He did so despite the odds and any suffering he might face. He wrestled with God.

Something amazing happened in the midst of Jacob's life threatening situation. Jacob had an encounter with God, which resulted in a huge change (Genesis 32:24-31). What's significant wasn't so much that Jacob encountered God. Rather, it was what Jacob did when he encountered God. He wrestled with God. There is no way one can win when wresting with God, but he dared to meet the challenge anyway. He wasn't going to give up. It didn't matter how long he had to do it, for he "…wrestled with him till daybreak" (v. 24). It didn't matter to him how much pain he was in, as "…his hip was wrenched as he wrestled…" (v. 25). He had decided that he wasn't going to give up until he got what he desired: "I will not let You go unless you bless me" (v. 26). He was determined not to settle for less.

In addition, Jacob continued wrestling, despite his immediate circumstances - that his brother Esau was on his way, and at any moment, Jacob was possibly going to lose everything he owned and loved, even his own life. He came to a place where, if it meant even forfeiting his life, he was willing to do it. And, at one point, Jacob said, "I saw God face to face, and yet my life was spared" (v. 30). And this is what God was looking for.

As a result, God blessed him, saying, "Your name will no longer be Jacob, but Israel, because you have struggled with God and with men and have overcome" (v. 28). And, after wrestling with God, Jacob did something his forefathers had never done: upon seeing Esau coming, he put his wives' and children's lives above his own, as "he himself went ahead" of them (Genesis 33:1-3).

As read earlier in this book, my father and grandfather never wrestled against the belief, "If I become a Christian, I'll be poor and miserable." Ironically, they settled for misery by not pursuing God, seeking help and failing to wrestle against their struggle. Thus, they allowed misery and settling for less to become a way of life. Even though I struggled with this same way of thinking for years, I somehow didn't let it stop me from seeking God and attempting to do His will, despite how I felt. Even when I fell down or gave up for a while, I always got back up and continued to seek God - no matter what He sent my way.

Maybe you've made some mistakes, or you've done some really stupid things. Maybe you gave up for a while. Maybe you had a setback or failure. Maybe you needed a break in order to regroup. The important thing is that, at some point, you get back in there. My challenge to you is to get back up, and get back to wrestling. No matter the setback, continue to wrestle against your generational iniquities. Continue to wrestle with God until He blesses you.

We cease wrestling with God when we no longer believe He is good, thus allowing our difficult circumstances to dictate His character. God allowed the circumstances in our lives – both good and bad. At times, we may not like our circumstances.

We may think them unfair. In some instances, we wonder if the Lord will ever deliver us. Complaining, blaming and making excuses will get us nowhere. Avoiding our circumstances only puts off the inevitable, and in the long run, it only empowers our fears, worries and suspicions. The only solution is to face our problems. Freedom from our fears only comes once we are willing to face them.

The Lord wants to see what we are willing to do, despite our circumstances. That's what wrestling is all about – that, no matter what life throws at us, we get back up and keep moving forward. Why? Because God is good, and we are not going to let our circumstances tell us otherwise. We must choose to continue wrestling no matter how long it takes, knowing there is a blessing that we will eventually get from the Lord. It is a blessing that we can't obtain by any other means.

When we cease wrestling, we make ourselves vulnerable to giving up completely. If we do this, we're actually trying to save our lives at the expense of something or someone else. In other words, we are unwilling to continue for fear that it will cost us. In reality, the Lord is asking us to come to a place where we are willing to let it cost us. Was this not what the Lord was attempting to do for the children of Israel while they were in the desert? For, whenever they feared that they would lose their lives, that is when they murmured and rebelled. Instead, God wanted them to be willing to trust Him and to die to themselves (and their fears), despite their circumstances. So, be willing to let it cost you, even if it means your very life.

God gave us our lives. He expects us to be good stewards of them. In so doing, He expects us to spend our lives, not to save them. "For whoever wishes to save his life will lose it; but whoever loses his life for My sake will find it" (Matthew 16:25). In God's economy, we find our life when we are willing to lose it.

I wonder: what might the Lord have had in store for Abraham and Isaac, had they been willing to forfeit their lives for sake of their wives, by trusting the Lord? As stated before, when a generational iniquity visits us, we aren't excused from any of the ways we give in to it. This is true even if we don't

121

realize there is a generational iniquity influencing us. Instead, we need to own up to any sinful responses we make, regardless of why. This is what confession and forgiveness are for, so we can get back on our feet and head back into the challenges before us.

Take, for instance, the times my son and I got into arguments. We were both responsible for our actions, regardless of any generational iniquities visiting us. It was our job to wrestle through them. And, it was more my job to do so than his, since I'm the father.

In the meantime, God wanted me to resist and to wrestle against the iniquities. He wanted me to be strengthened in my ability to resist the influence and to persevere in my relationship with my son, despite there being a generational iniquity visiting us. He wanted to teach me humility, to be able to admit when I'm wrong and ask forgiveness of my son. He wanted to teach me persistence, for me to keep pursuing my son, heading into the relationship, even when I made mistakes and was wrong. It was also important for my son to learn by my example, especially how to recover from mistakes. To be honest, all of this was very difficult, and I was by no means perfect. However, I will say that I kept getting back up again and again, heading into my relationship with my son. And, eventually, it paid off.

If I had not resisted and gave into sinful responses, I would have eventually justified my own behavior and labeled my son as the problem. Even worse, I would have ended up giving in to the generational animosity, focusing it on my son and, thus, reinforcing the generational iniquity. Thus, I would have ensured that it would pass onto the next generation. But, through resisting, I was eventually able to recognize and identify what my son and I were really struggling against. And, through prayer, the visitation of the generational iniquity was removed.

Things to Consider

- What would God have you wrestle against?
- What will it cost you to continue to wrestle against it?
- What is the worst that could happen, were you not to give up? Would that result really be so bad?
- On the other hand, what troubles might come upon your descendants if you do give up?
- What is in store for you, personally, if you choose to not give up?
- Are you willing to surrender to the Lord "the worst that could happen," and trust Him with your life? If so, do so now, in prayer.

The Prayer of Jabez

Jabez was more honorable than his brothers,
and his mother named him Jabez saying,
"Because I bore him with pain."
Now Jabez called on the God of Israel, saying,
"Oh that You would bless me indeed and enlarge my border,
and that Your hand might be with me,
and that You would keep me from harm
that it may not pain me!"
And God granted him what he requested.
I Chronicles 4:9-10

Jabez

As we look through the various generations in the Bible, I want to take a brief moment to point out Jabez. Jabez stands out amongst his generations.

Jabez had a painful past, starting with his birth! His birth was such a painful experience for his mother that she decided to name him Jabez, which means, "pain." Can you imagine being remembered for your mother's pain in giving birth to you? It makes one wonder if Jabez felt that he wasn't a joy to his mother.

And what about every time someone called his name? "Hey Jabez [pain], have you done your chores?" Again, wouldn't this reinforce the lie that it was somehow Jabez's fault that his mother went through so much pain? And, over time, wouldn't this begin to make him think that he *was* a pain, that it was just who he was – that he was destined to be a pain?

How about every time Jabez had to introduce himself?

"Hi. What's your name?"

"Jabez [pain]."

Which only begs the question of: "So, how did you get that name?!"

Once again, Jabez would have to tell his story, only to remind himself that he wasn't a blessing to his mother, but a pain. In addition, why did his father allow him to be given such a name? Imagine what other things Jabez might have endured growing up – being teased, having to avoid people, and always having to explain himself.

Yet, despite all of this, Jabez decided that he wasn't going to let his past affect his future. He wasn't going to let the implied blame and troubles of others rule him. Rather, he decided he would overcome them. He chose not to live up to his given name. And, in so doing, he sought the Lord, asking Him to bless him.

And eventually Jabez not only overcame his past, but also he prevented a generational iniquity from starting, and left behind a legacy of encouragement for people like you and me. He was considered "more honorable" (I Chronicles 4:9) for the simple reason that he sought the Lord so as to overcome his past. And the Lord granted his request.

And so, thereafter, whenever Jabez introduced himself and was asked, "How did you get that name?" he now had a different answer to give. From then on, he could say, "Let me tell you what the Lord did for me..." He could then share how the Lord redeemed his name and his past. It became his testimony of God answering prayer in his life!

Jabez's decision to overcome his past by seeking the Lord is an example to all of us. His prayer isn't a formula for success, as if we could make the Lord answer our requests, nor is it something for us to repeat word for word. Rather, his prayer is an example of what we should do with the things that have pained us in our lives.

Jabez's prayer contains elements that were important to him, for which he sought the Lord. Rather than letting his past rule his life, he allowed it to motivate him to seek the Lord. Rather than letting his past determine his future, he asked God to bless his future, despite his past.

We have no idea how long Jabez prayed – a few days, several weeks, or even many months. Perhaps Jabez prayed for years until, one day, he received what he requested.

I have had the Lord answer prayers within the same day. I have also had Him answer them before I even asked! And, yet, I have had prayers that took years before He answered. I even have prayers that I have been asking for over 25 years, and God still has not answered them. The key is this: are you willing to seek Him in prayer, despite your past, despite how hard it is and has been, and no matter how long it takes? Jabez was.

My challenge to you isn't that you pray Jabez's prayer. Rather, what would be *your* prayer to the Lord? What is your pain? What is your past? What changes do you want to make in your family line? What is it that you want to overcome that no matter what, you will seek the Lord about, until He answers you?

The choice is yours. Do you want to go with the flow from generation to generation? Or, do you want to stand out from your generations? In seeking the Lord for change, not only will you be blessed, but also, you will pass on blessings to subsequent generations.

 Things to Consider
- What are you past "pains"?
- What is it that you would like to see the Lord do in your life, and change for future generations?
- In light of your past, what would your prayer to the Lord be?
  - Write it down.
  - Begin seeking the Lord, in prayer, concerning your request.
  - Record any time the Lord gives you encouragement, confirmation, wisdom and direction concerning your prayer.
  - Continue the process until the Lord answers.

126

Generational Reconcilers

So I gave my attention to the Lord God to seek Him by prayer
and supplications, with fasting, sackcloth and ashes. I prayed to
the LORD my God and confessed and said,
"Alas, O Lord, the great and awesome God, who
keeps His covenant and lovingkindness for those
who love Him and keep His commandments, we
have sinned, committed iniquity, acted wickedly
and rebelled, even turning aside from Your
commandments and ordinances. Moreover, we
have not listened to Your servants the prophets,
who spoke in Your name to our kings, our princes,
our fathers and all the people of the land."
Daniel 9:3-6

No One Will Stop It

While writing this book, I received a very encouraging
report from a friend. The Lord had strategically
involved him in exposing hidden, historical corruption in his
city. And, after many months of prayer, it was now being
undone!

A little over a year ago, I called my friend, only to hear
some disturbing news. After praying with him and getting off
of the phone, I decided I would call him every so often to see
how things were going, so as to provide encouragement and
prayer. Yet, whenever I did, I learned that it was going from
bad to worse. The following is a summary of just a few of the
things that had happened.

It all began with a building project, on the land adjacent to
my friend's property of several acres. He went outside one day,
only to discover that someone had bulldozed his fence and was
beginning to grade part of his property. Thinking that there was

a misunderstanding, he very nicely pointed this out to the man on the bulldozer, only to be treated harshly, as if my friend was the one doing wrong. Shocked by this, he contacted the company that was doing the project. Yet again, he was treated in the same manner. He was even threatened by them. So, he contacted the city building department, but they did nothing about it. This went on and on: no matter who he contacted, he was either treated harshly or ignored.

When my friend attempted to take the building company to court, each time he hired a lawyer, at some point the lawyer would quit. It was as if they were being scared off. In addition, the building company knew that, if they dragged the court case on and on, eventually my friend would run out of money and would give up. Several times, his property and his life were threatened. He received threatening messages on his answering machine. Once, someone took a shot at him while he was on his roof. Fortunately, they missed. When he reported it to the police, they did nothing.

My friend began to realize that there were those in places of leadership in his city who were in on this corruption. In addition, the building company was forcing all of the people in the adjacent trailer park to leave without due compensation, and many of them had nowhere to go. And yet, none of the city's leadership would stop the building company.

As my friend researched further, he found that this particular company had a reputation of bullying property owners and blatantly violating the law, but no one ever stopped them. Only five years prior, a reporter for the local newspaper was found dead in a lake. Was it coincidental that, at the time, the reporter had been writing an article that exposed complaints about the very same building company? In addition, there was a young woman who was said to have committed suicide. This occurred around the same time she was to testify about wrongdoings concerning the building company. However, no one investigated any further, despite the evidence.

This ongoing experience had brought unwanted and unwarranted stress into the lives of my friend and his wife. Their lives, property and animals were being threatened. It was costing them lots of money that they might never get back. It was stealing from what was once a peaceful life. And it looked like things were only going to get worse.

One day, when I called my friend again, I told him that this corruption felt like a historical iniquity, committed by those in city leadership years ago. The theme was: "There are those who will do whatever they want, even it means going above the law, and those who could stop it, won't." So, I asked if he knew the history of his city, and he did. As he shared, it was amazing to hear how the very founding of his city was just like the present situation! In short, his city was founded by force, without going through the proper legal means, and yet, no one did anything about it.

So, my friend and I began to confess the iniquities of the founding leaders of his city, and of those on the county level who did nothing to stop them. We also confessed the iniquities of the present leaders and the building company. We asked that the Lord would have mercy and intervene, and especially that He would bring justice to those who couldn't defend themselves. After praying, we committed to continue praying in like manner. We did this for many months. Finally, one day, my friend got a phone message. It was from officials of his state.

The state officials said that the issue had come to their attention, and, not only were they going to investigate, but also they would do so pro bono! Since this first phone call, other state departments have stepped in as well.

For the first time in the history of my friend's city, those who have the means to stop the corruption are beginning to do so. The Lord was not only addressing the historical iniquity over my friend's city, but He also began to deal with the corruption and to restore the city's redemptive purposes!

As Christians, the Lord calls all of us to participate, in some manner, in His kingdom work in this world. It is our privilege to be a part of the amazing things He is doing and is going to do. We have all been called to be obedient and faithful to Him in all we undertake. In the midst of this, God often assigns specific tasks for each of us to accomplish. In this way we work as a team, directly and indirectly helping one another and impacting our world.

For instance, all of us are to share the good news of what Jesus has done in our lives, but some are called to specialize in this. Such individuals are called evangelists, as they do this on a regular basis. We are all to worship the Lord, but some specialize in leading us in worship. We are all to pray, but the Lord directs some to do this more than others, and in specific ways. They are called intercessors.

All of us have the privilege and responsibility to confess generational iniquities whenever we are made aware of them. But the Lord has some of us doing this more than others. It is a form of intercession. Such people are known as generational reconcilers. Daniel was such a man. So was Nehemiah.

When Steven spoke before the high priest and those present, he shared the history of the Israelites, and stated, "...you are doing just as your fathers did" (Acts 7:61). He was confronting their iniquities and those of their forefathers. God through Steven was giving them an opportunity to be generational reconcilers, allowing them to be the ones to confess the iniquities and repent. In the past when their forefathers were confronted, they persecuted and killed the messengers (Acts 7:62). At that moment they were in the same situation as their forefathers - they were being confronted by a man of God concerning their iniquities. That moment was a gift from God to be set free. They could either resist the generational influence and repent, or give in to it. Unfortunately, they did the later and they stoned Steven.

When I was a child, a friend and I would collect black sand. We would each take a magnet and drag it under the dirt. As we did this, the magnet would attract the black sand. Upon bringing the magnet out of the dirt, we would scrape off the black sand and put it in a jar.

Many years ago, the Lord gave me a vision. I saw a large magnet being dragged through the dirt, collecting black sand. The Lord told me that I was like that magnet, and the black sand was generational iniquities. He told me that, as I would go through life, many of my family's generational iniquities would be "attracted" to me. This would happen as I had experiences in life that were similar to those of my ancestors, thus invoking a visitation of a generational iniquity. This was so I could identify and confess them, in order to break their generational influence. I have met other people to whom the Lord has assigned this task as well.

What the Lord typically does is to put me in circumstances that will allow the visitation of a generational iniquity to occur. I then experience its influence and attempt to endure it. During the season of endurance, I seek the Lord in prayer, asking for insight into the historical cause. Once identified, I then pray through the historical iniquity until its influence lifts off. This is how I know I have completed each generational assignment from the Lord.

Each assignment usually has a different theme or is another layer of a prior theme. Sometimes, I have more than one assignment at the same time, or similar assignments will overlap. From time to time, the Lord gives me a break. Some assignments have lasted as little as a few days to several weeks, and some have been as long as many months. I have some that have gone on for years.

I usually know I have another assignment when I begin to recognize, in my life, the evidence of the influence of a generational iniquity. There are only two ways to find relief. One is to head into the assignment, which is not always easy, but it is rewarding, and it's the wise thing to do. The other way isn't wise. It is to tolerate the influence, and eventually, to give in to it. Toleration, minimization, denial and compromise won't make it go away. They only allow it to continue influencing, despite one's attempts to ignore it. Worse yet, one will begin to go numb in his or her spiritual discernment.

To be honest, most of the time, it isn't fun being a generational reconciler. Life doesn't stop just because you are bearing under a generational influence. You still have to go to work, pay bills, love your neighbor and tend to your other responsibilities. The Lord expects you to be mature and to grow in the midst of your assignments. Bearing under a generational influence is no excuse for bad behavior. In addition, most people don't understand what you are going through. Therefore, it's important to find those who do understand, to keep one another accountable and to pray for one another.

At times, being a generational reconciler is a form of suffering. This suffering is often at the expense of your circumstances, possessions, finances, opportunities and relationships. The generational influence interferes with and distracts from these. Depending upon the influence, you must often wrestle against negative feelings such as loneliness, doubt, fear and disappointment, to name a few. And you must do so while continuing to manage your daily life. Completing an assignment will cost time, energy, sleep and resources while you resist. Sometimes, you will give up or give in to the influence. But, at some point, I encourage you to get back up, receive God's grace and forgiveness, and begin dealing with it again, asking the Lord to reveal the historical iniquity.

If you can relate to any of this, be encouraged. The Lord has given you such an assignment because He knows you have (and will have) what it takes to complete it. I want to encourage you that, no matter what it costs, it is worth it. While in the midst of an assignment, you may not understand how this could be, but someday, you will, for we know that it is working something good for God's purposes and glory. In God's kingdom, nothing great comes without great sacrifice. And, just as our Lord gave His life for us, why should anything less be expected of us? (I Peter 4:12-13). In the end, all that we go through will bring great honor and glory to our Lord.

My friend who endured suffering from the iniquity of his city is a generational reconciler. His most recent assignment had to do with his city. Many years ago, the Lord strategically placed him in that very city on a specific piece of land without his knowing what the Lord had planned. Then, when the time was right, the Lord purposely engaged him in the influence of the city's historical iniquity. As my friend (a citizen, and thus a representative, of that city) and I confessed the iniquities, the Lord began to undo all that had been done. All of this happened because of my friend's willingness to trust the Lord, pay the cost (even if it meant his life, possessions and money), intercede and not quit.

During the writing of this book, a friend invited me to participate in something the Lord has allowed him and a team of others to do. God gives them assignments, leading them to reconcile unresolved historical events between leaders and nations. As the Lord leads them to specific regions, they meet with various leaders there. Together, they seek the Lord for insight into any historical iniquities. They then encourage the leaders, who are representatives of that region, to reconcile their differences, seek unity and pray through any historical iniquities. As a result, leaders from various countries and churches have been reconciled. In many instances, it has brought about healing, transformation and unity for the first time in many years. Generational strongholds over specific cities and nations have been removed. And, in some cases, it has even brought about changes in government! My friend and his team are generational reconcilers, operating on a national level.

Your Assignment

So, what is your assignment? Your assignment is right where you are. It is in the place God has put you and in the midst of the relationships you have there. It's in the present circumstances you are in and the era in which you exist. Though your present assignment may include being a generational reconciler, we are all called to bring about reconciliation and to lead others to reconciliation with God (II Corinthians 5:18-20). Your assignment involves the people the Lord has put in your life.

133

The Lord has strategically placed you right where you are so He can accomplish what He wants to do through you. Everything from your nationality, gender, age, talents, location and more are exactly what is needed to do what the Lord wants to do through you. You are a son/daughter, citizen, friend, neighbor and employee. Perhaps you are roommate, student, business owner, leader or member of some organization. These are your spheres of influence. As you are faithful within them, God knows you will be faithful in other tasks. Therefore, He will eventually give you more favor and expand your influence. So, be faithful where you are. No task in the body of Christ is trivial, and no assignment given by the Lord is impossible to complete. For He sees your faithfulness, even in the little things, and with Him, all things are possible.

 Things to Consider
- What assignments has the Lord given you?
- Are there any assignments that you have avoided or given up on? Why? If so, confess this to the Lord, and ask Him to help you complete your assignment.
- Take an assessment of where the Lord has placed you. Ask Him how He would have you be faithful where you are.
- Are you in a place or relationship where you shouldn't be? If so, ask the Lord for forgiveness, and repent by asking where you should be. Know that the Lord will redeem any wrong you have done.
- Are there some aspects about yourself and where the Lord has you, for which you have been ungrateful? If so, ask the Lord for forgiveness, and offer these things to Him, asking Him to use them for His redemptive purposes.

Generational Blessings

Their offspring will be known among the nations,
And their descendants in the midst of the peoples.
All who see them will recognize them because they are the
offspring whom the LORD has blessed.
Isaiah 61:9

Impart by Example

A while back, I was reviewing my life, reflecting upon my many apparent disappointments. These were times when, despite my efforts, optimism and investment of time and energy, things did not turn out as I had hoped. They involved business ventures, ministry opportunities and even relationships. At the end of many of these experiences, I had been left feeling discouraged and exhausted, often doubting myself, my faith and God. Yes, I experienced some successes too. But, at this time of reflection, I was primarily focusing on my failures. I had hoped to pass on a legacy of success and opportunity to my children, but all I could see at the time were my own failures and disappointments.

Without going into details, I shared with my son how I had hoped so much more for him, concerning these "failed" opportunities. Yet, to my surprise, he said, "Dad, it's because of your and Mom's faith in God that I have my faith in God." What blessed me as well was when my daughter said something similar. She said, "I've never once felt deprived. What mattered was that I always felt loved and cared for. Your and Mom's faith was imparted to me, as was your life example – living it out daily."

Man's measure of success is not the same as God's. The Lord evaluates our success based on how we loved others and how faithful we were. In God's economy, this is what makes a difference in our children's lives, and this is a generational legacy we can pass on to them!

There are several ways to pass on generational blessings.

Live in the Fear of the Lord
> How blessed is the man who fears the Lord,
> Who greatly delights in His commandments.
> His descendants will be mighty on earth;
> The generation of the upright will be blessed.
> Psalms 112:2-3

It is a promise to us that, when we choose to fear the Lord, our children will be blessed. In Luke 1:50, Mary, Jesus' mother, quotes Psalms 107:7. This verse speaks of the Lord: "His mercy is upon generation after generation toward those who fear Him." The promise is that He will extend mercy to our descendants as we live a life in the fear of the Lord. What an awesome blessing to pass onto our children!

To fear the Lord is a choice. It is a choice to live in such a way that we recognize that He is in absolute control and that He is who He says He is. Thus, we make decisions based upon His character. Fearing the Lord does not mean living a perfect life, but living a life of honoring, obeying and submitting to Him, even though we do fail and make mistakes.

I love that saying: "God is good all the time." One of the ways we live in fear of the Lord is to always let God's character interpret our circumstances, rather than letting our circumstances interpret God's character. If you find yourself in a difficult situation, question your circumstances, but not whether God is good. Fear the Lord, not your struggles. In so doing, your children will be blessed!

Build Generational Character
> Then they will rebuild the ancient ruins,
> They will raise up the former devastations;
> And they will repair the ruined cities,
> The desolations of many generations.
> Isaiah 61:4

As shared in previous chapters, it is important to build generational character back into the family line. Removing generational influence is significant, but replacing it with generational character takes it one step further.

When we overcome, we gain authority concerning an issue or task. This imparts the belief to our children: "Well, if my dad (or mom) can do it, then so can I!" Perhaps they will not do the same accomplishments as us – like writing a book. But, they can be inspired by what we did do, overcoming their own obstacles as they pursue their dreams. In addition, they will be able to take it further than us as we have made a clearer path in life for them.

What is true of us all as parents is that there are many things we have the opportunity to do that may never be noticed, but such things will make an impact on our children's lives. Not only will they be blessed by whatever you overcome, they will also be by your example, believing that they too can overcome the challenges they will face in their lives.

Speak Blessings
> Permit the children to come to Me; do not hinder them;
> for the kingdom of God belongs to such as these...
> And He took them in His arms and began blessing them,
> laying His hands on them.
> Mark 10:14, 19

Jesus blessed children - and so should we. Even more so, we, as parents, should bless the presence of the Lord in their lives, permitting Him to be an active part of all they do.

When the Lord designed parents, He gave them the power to speak into their children's lives. Through their words, parents

137

have the ability to empower their children and to speak into their future. The significance of parents' words is more powerful than those of anyone else in a child's life.

When our children hear such words, it helps them believe that they can achieve at tasks they may not have otherwise thought they could. It allows them to know that they have a purpose in life. In imparts a sense that they have a special future. Specifically, speaking good words over a child's potential can make a huge difference. Such words provide strength that can be drawn upon when life becomes challenging.

In Genesis 49, Jacob spoke words of blessing over his sons. When he did so, he spoke directly to them and in the presence of others. What is interesting is that Scripture says Jacob "blessed them, every one with the blessing appropriate to him."

You don't have to wait for a word from God before you speak into your children's lives. Do it now. Do it often. Do it whenever you think of something affirming about them. And then, do it again – even if you find that you're repeating yourself.

When you impart words of blessing and affirmation to your children, it sets in motion an influence, not only in their lives, but also in their children's lives. Think about it: if you do it for them, they are more likely to do it for their children, who are more likely to do it for their children as well.

Numbers 26:24-26 is a well-known blessing, which is as follows:

> The Lord bless you, and keep you;
> The Lord make His face shine on you,
> And be gracious to you;
> The Lord lift up His countenance on you,
> And give you peace.

The priests were instructed by the Lord to bless the children of Israel by saying the above blessing over them. The Lord said that whenever they did this, "they shall invoke My name on the sons of Israel, and I then will bless them" (Numbers 26:27).

The Lord desires to bless you and your children, but He is waiting to be called upon to do so. The picture that I envision is the Lord full of great delight in wanting to bless, as if He almost cannot contain Himself, while waiting to be asked to do so. Why does He wait? For one, by design, He uses those who provide spiritual covering, such as parents, to bless those under them. But also, He wants us, as parents, to have the privilege of participating in this wonderful experience - for it to be our delight as well. Therefore, in order to not miss out on this incredible blessing, bless your children's lives, asking the Lord to bless them and be in their lives.

One other important way to bless your children is to pray for them. Pray for their daily lives as well as their future. And, from time to time be sure to pray with them.

Deal with Generational Iniquities

We have sinned, committed iniquity,
acted wickedly and rebelled, even turning aside from
Your commandments and ordinances.
Moreover, we have not listened to
Your servants the prophets,
who spoke in Your name to our kings, our princes,
our fathers and all the people of the land.
Daniel 9:5-6

This almost goes without saying, since the testimonies in this book illustrate the results of dealing with generational iniquities. Our children will have their struggles and challenges. Yet, how much better will it be for them if we, as parents, do our part to remove negative influences from their lives.

So, I encourage you to complete your God-given assignments. Head into whatever challenges life gives you. At this time, you may have no idea why you are going through what you are experiencing, but, inevitably, it will make an impact on subsequent generations. Break the generational patterns of iniquity and remove their influences.

Honor the Previous Generations

Honor your father and mother
(which is the first commandment with a promise),
so that it may be well with you,
and that you may live long on the earth.
Ephesians 4:2-3

Honoring your father and mother is a commandment that comes with a promise. You will be blessed for doing it - life will go well for you. So this is definitely a blessing you don't want to miss out on.

When we honor our parents, we pass the blessing of doing this on to our children. This becomes part of their heritage. In addition, they will be more inclined to honor us as well, because this is what we have instilled into them by example.

One of the ways you honor your parents is by forgiving them for any offenses they have done. When you forgive them, you are saying that they do not owe you - to make up for what they did not do as well as for what hurtful things they did do. This frees you to no longer be under the oppression of such hurts, and to move forward in receiving healing from the Lord. It is not our place to hold them accountable for what they did or did not do. Their stewardship of their lives is before God. When we forgive them, we honor them by releasing them to God, which in turn sets us free.

You also honor your parents by being thankful for the good things they did and gave you as well as any positive character traits they had. No matter how imperfect your parents and even your grandparents may have been, there are always things you can find to be thankful for. It could be such things as the uniqueness of your nationality, the things they attempted and accomplished, or the few to many good things they taught you. Perhaps they had a love for art, science, animals or humanitarian efforts. They may have had a talent for music, gardening, business, etc. These are part of your heritage.

Here are a few examples from my own life.

Even though I came from a family with two generations of divorce, both of my parents were adventurous. They loved trying new things, traveling and exploring. This is something I have inherited, and so have my children. My mom taught me how to cook, and I enjoy cooking to this day. As for character, she has always shown respect toward others, even when others have not been so nice to her. My father taught me how to use tools and how to fix things. As a result, I'm not afraid to take things apart and fix broken things myself. As for character, he was always a good host and hospitable toward others.

Honoring my parents, I have expressed thanks to them on many occasions for such things. I have done this in person as well as through cards on special occasions. Since my father passed away several years ago, from time to time I express thanks to God for the good things he did. This is especially true on days when I remember him or realize some new aspect about him.

We can also honor our parents by doing things to express our thanks to them. We can celebrate their birthdays, call them from time to time, and take them out to dinner. We can also bless them by praying for them, asking them for advice, and helping them out when they need support or assistance with something.

Whenever you get the chance to say something about your parents, share about the good things. In this way you are actively and publicly honoring them. When I was given the privilege to officiate at my father's funeral, this is exactly what I did. I shared many of the good things about my dad. In addition, I even encouraged others to share what they appreciated about him. I encourage you to take advantage of every opportunity to speak well about your parents.

Sometimes when you pray through generational iniquities, the Lord will reveal certain honorable deeds and attributes about your ancestors. When He does, give thanks to the Lord for these things. These are part of your inheritance.

Behind every generational iniquity there was a good thing that was intended to happen if the ancestor had not committed the iniquity. Unfortunately, they had failed to walk in what was meant for their family line. Though you cannot make up for what they did or did not do, you can choose to pick-up

141

where they left off. You can decide to make right decisions in your life.

Honoring the previous generations is important for several reasons. For one, as stated before, there is a blessing that comes with this - that life may go well with you! Also, it allows you to see the humanity of your ancestors - that they did good things too, causing you to not just focus on their iniquities. In addition, it gives you a sense of who you are and where you came from. This allows you to know where you are going. It provides a sense of direction - that this is what you were put on this earth to do.

One last thing - we do not honor our ancestors by worshipping them, as is practiced in some cultures. This is forbidden by the Lord, as we are to only worship Him. Worshipping our ancestors always leads to bondage. We do not live under the control and fear of our ancestors. Our destiny is in the hands of the Lord, not them. The blessing that comes when we honor our parents comes directly from the Lord, not our ancestors. We are free to receive this blessing from the Lord whether our ancestors were good or bad and regardless of whether or not they were pleased with us.

Leave a Legacy
... which we have heard and known,
And our fathers have told us.
We will not conceal them from their children,
But tell to the generation to come the praises of the Lord,
And His strength and His wondrous works that He has done.
For He established a testimony in Jacob,
And appointed a law in Israel, Which he commanded our
fathers, That they should make them known to their children;
That the generation to come might know them, even the
children that should be born;
Who should arise and tell them to their children,
That they might set their hope in God,
And not forget the works of God,
But keep his commandments.
Psalms 78:3-7
142

When I decided, years ago, to write my first book, it seemed like an overwhelming task. I had never done anything like it before. As I got further into the project, I learned about the many details that go into publishing a book. Though it was a lot of work, the key was that I kept going, one day at a time. Eventually, after much perseverance, I published my first book: *Pray Through It.*[22] Many blessings have come as a result of this. For one, I experienced the joy of completing a task and seeing others blessed by it. Also, because of all that I learned through the process, it was so much easier to write my second book. Lastly, the experience that I gained has enabled me to encourage and help others who are considering writing a book.

One day, I sent a copy of my book to my brother-in-law. He showed it to his daughter, saying, "Look what uncle Rob wrote!" A few weeks later, I received a packet in the mail. To my delight, in it was something my niece had created. She had drawn several illustrations in crayon, creating a wonderful story about two little girls. Her father had assisted by writing out her words for the story on each page. Lastly, she bound it together with staples. She had created her very own book! It was as if she realized, "Well, if Uncle Rob can write a book, then so can I!" And, sure enough, she did!

If I was able to impact my niece in such a way, just think how much of more of an impact your choices can and will make upon your own children! By the way, my daughter and I have since published a book together,[23] and she even has some ideas for a book of her own!

What you persevere through, no matter how insignificant and unseen it may seem, you leave a legacy for your children. Whatever conquests and things you go through with the Lord, you leave this as an inheritance for your children.

In addition, tell your children of the things the Lord has done in your life and the lives of others. And, from time to

---

[22] *Pray Through It* (ISBN: 987-0-976354-90-1) available at Amazon.com
[23] *Garage Sale Mania* (ISBN: 978-0-9763549-5-6) also available at Amazon.com

time, tell them again. This will cause then to anticipate that the Lord can and will do great things in their lives.

Be One Who Restores and Rebuilds the Generations

One day while in the synagogue (Luke 4:16-21), Jesus read from Isaiah 61:1-2a, which says:

> The Spirit of the Lord is upon Me,
> Because He anointed Me to preach the gospel to the poor.
> He has sent Me to proclaim release to the captives,
> And recovery of sight to the blind,
> To set free those who are oppressed,
> To proclaim the favorable year of the Lord.

Then, Jesus said something amazing: "Today, this Scripture is fulfilled in your midst" (Luke 4:21). What is wonderful is that you and I are the recipients of all these things He came to do! Were we not all in some way in need of His help, especially for Him to be our Savior?

As we continue on and read Isaiah 61:2b-3, we discover even more of what Jesus came to do:

> And the day of vengeance of our God;
> To comfort all who mourn,
> To grant those who mourn in Zion,
> Giving them a garland instead of ashes,
> The oil of gladness instead of mourning,
> The mantle of praise instead of a spirit of fainting.
> So they will be called oaks of righteousness,
> The planting of the Lord, that He may be glorified.

But, there is even more in store for us! The "they" in Isaiah 4:4 is speaking of those of us who have been recipients of the Lord's ministry. It is through us that the following great promise is made:

144

They will rebuild the ancient ruins
and restore the places long devastated;
they will renew the ruined cities
that have been devastated for generations.

Therefore, know that no matter how seemingly insignificant or great it may appear, you have been called in some manner to restore the generations. You can and do make a difference!

Things to Consider

- The next time you confess in prayer a generation iniquity, be sure to do the following as well concerning your ancestors:
  - Identify any good attributes and things they did.
  - Spend time giving thanks to the Lord for these things.
  - If they are still alive, honor them by finding some ways to express thanks to them for these good things.
- What are four or more things that you can be thankful for concerning your parents? Spend time giving thanks to God for these things.
- What is something you can do to express thanks to your parents?
- What are some specific words of encouragement that you can speak over your children? Make a list. Tell them what you have written down.
- Is there an area in your life in which you have allowed your circumstances to tempt you to believe that God is not as good as you had once believed? If so, talk to God about it. Ask Him for forgiveness, and ask Him to help you to believe, despite your circumstances.
- What is the most recent challenge God has brought into your life? Choose to see it as something God wants you to overcome, so you can leave a legacy for your children. Ask God to help you.

Supplemental Information

Questions about Generational Iniquity

Question: *How important is it to know from which parent a generational iniquity is inherited?*

It isn't necessary to know this in order to pray through a generational iniquity. What is important is identifying the iniquity and confessing it.

Question: *Do we need to know the exact generation of the source of a generational iniquity?*

It really doesn't make a difference. Knowing historical dates (or time periods), names of people, and even the specific side of the family is important only if the Lord reveals such things. What *is* important is knowing what the generational iniquity was, because this is what is confessed in prayer.

Question: *If I pray through something generational, do my children need to pray through it as well?*

It may not be necessary, since only one person needs to confess the generational iniquity. However, there is something powerful in more than one family member confessing. In Ezra 9, the men, women and children all repented together. Also, there are certain benefits of having your children pray with you. For one, it helps to instruct them about the significance of generational iniquities, as well as the importance of recognizing and praying through them. It gives them a model for how to pray through generational iniquities. It also demonstrates to them the importance of not letting a sin become an iniquity.

If you have allowed a generational iniquity to become a part of your life, it is very important to confess the ways you have done so. If your children have done so as well, so should they. In addition, it is important to put into practice new ways of living (opposite to the iniquity) so as to create new and desirable habits.

Question: *What about the influence of generational iniquities coming from other relatives, such as uncles, aunts, cousins, etc.?*

Though you are related to your uncles, aunts, etc., you didn't descend from them. Therefore, the influence of any of their iniquities doesn't visit you. But, if you confess any generational iniquities from your forefathers, this can have a positive impact on any relatives who are descendants of them.

Question: *What about praying blessings so as to counteract a generational iniquity?*

Praying blessings upon others is what God would have us do regardless, and even upon our enemies (Matthew 5:44). This is something I highly encourage people to do, especially after a generational iniquity has been confessed. However, praying blessings won't remove a generational iniquity. You cannot overcome a generational iniquity by flooding a person with prayers of blessing, as the Bible makes it clear that generational iniquities are only removed through confession.

Question: *What if I am not sure that the information I think God gave me, or the family history I have been told, is really what happened?*

If you don't pray through it, you will never know. If you do pray, and nothing happens, there is no harm done. But, if you do pray through something and a change results, then you know that something was indeed true about the information you have received. So, it's better to have prayed through something than not to have prayed and be left wondering.

When identifying and praying through generational iniquities, we aren't trying to prove every detail of what really happened historically. Instead, we take what we do have, offer it to God, in prayer, and see what happens. The Bible says that we see dimly, and that we know in part, but someday, we will know fully (I Corinthians 13:12).

As we seek God, He will give us just the details we need so we can bring the influence of the generational iniquities to an end. So, don't allow your lack of absolute certainty hinder you from praying through what has been revealed to you.

Question: *What about II Corinthians 5:17, which says that, as a Christian, you are a "new creature"?*

When you became a Christian, you became a new creature. Prior to this, you had no means of reconciling with God. But, now that you are a Christian, you do.

The passage is specifically speaking to Christians. The verses that follow state, that as a Christian (as a new creature), you have been given the ministry of reconciliation (II Corinthians 5:18). Furthermore, out of this new relationship with God, you are instructed to "be reconciled to God" (v. 20). And what is to be reconciled? You are to reconcile your heart to God, through confession of your sins, transgressions and iniquities with God. This includes generational iniquities.

Question: *What of Ezekiel 18:20, which says that "the son shall not bear the iniquity of the father"?*

When you read verse 20, you need to read the entire chapter. In the days of Ezekiel, an erroneous saying was circulating, which many people believed to be truth. This erroneous proverb was: "The fathers have eaten sour grapes, and the children's teeth are set on edge." This isn't a proverb that God had given. Drawing from the whole passage, the meaning of this saying was: "The sons are punished for the wrongs of the fathers." So, God confronted this erroneous teaching through Ezekiel. Jeremiah 31:29-30 also addresses this very same issue.

When you read verse 20 in the context of the whole chapter of Ezekiel 18, it's clear by the proceeding verses what is meant by "The son shall not bear" – that is, the son shall not die for his father's iniquities. This passage is actually clarifying that children aren't to be punished (in this case, by dying) for the iniquities of their fathers. In addition, this passage is making it clear that each person is accountable for his own sins against God: "The soul that sinneth, it shall die" (Ezekiel 18:20). Therefore, the visiting of the iniquities of the fathers isn't a punishment from God upon the children. Rather, it is the outworking of the natural law of sowing and reaping.

Question: *I thought we were no longer under the Old Covenant. So, why do we need to confess generational iniquities?*
Yes, as Christians, we are under a New Covenant (I Corinthians 11:25). It is the blood of Jesus, and no longer the blood of lambs, which cleanses all sins. Whenever we sin, we are to confess it in order to receive what Jesus did so as to stop the reaping. When Jesus suffered, died and rose from the dead, He paid for all our sins, transgressions and iniquities. Through our confession, we receive the benefit of what He did (I John 1:9; James 4:16), which stops of negative reaping. It is no different for generational iniquities. Just as personal sins, they need to be confessed as well.

Question: *But I have never had children and/or don't plan on having any. So, why should I pray through generational iniquities if there is no one to be set free in later generations?*
The Lord wouldn't have us do something unless it had some divine purpose. For one, praying through generational iniquities sets you free. There might be certain opportunities the Lord has for you, but, until you have completed your present assignments, He won't let you move on. In addition, when you pray through generational iniquities, it sets free any relatives who are related to the ancestor who committed the iniquity. Also, you will grow in sensitivity and maturity concerning generational iniquities, and the Lord can then use you to minister to others.

Question: *What about when Paul said, "...forgetting those things which are behind" (Philippians 3:13)?*
Paul wasn't talking about anything generational. He was speaking very specifically about his accomplishments, training and knowledge, none of which compares with knowing Christ. Rather than dwell on any accomplishments, losses and past regrets, Paul made it his primary goal to: "... press toward the

149

mark for the prize of the high calling of God in Christ Jesus."
(Philippians 3:14)

Question: *What about when the Lord blessed the generations of Abraham and David?*

There are instances in which the Lord imparted a specific blessing upon a person's family line. He did this to accomplish His divine purposes. Such examples are Abraham and David.

In Abraham's case, the Lord made a promise to him before he had ever demonstrated his faith in the Lord. The Lord said to Abraham, "In you all the nations of the earth shall be blessed" (Genesis 12:3). In David's case, the Lord blessed David's generations concerning his rule and reign. (II Samuel 7:1-17).

In both instances, these promises were not something they had earned. Yet, knowing of their faithfulness, the Lord secured a generational blessing, which ultimately referred to Jesus Christ, the Son of Man, who is a direct descendant of Abraham and David.

Question: *What about reincarnation? Couldn't what I'm sensing be from a past life?*

Reincarnation is the belief that one's life is a cycle of death and rebirth. In other words, one has lived previous lives and will be reborn, to live again, after death. There are variations of this belief for different people and religions, but this is the basic premise. Some people have come to believe in reincarnation because of what they were taught, or merely out of ignorance. But reincarnation isn't biblical.

There are some who believe in reincarnation, basing it upon certain experiences they claim to have had. They say that they believe they lived previously in another life because they have had revelations of past experiences. In some cases, it is as if they have memories of past lives, or they just have a sense that it is true for them. It is as if these experiences were their own. It is as if there is something inside that resonates, telling them that there is some truth to what they are sensing. So, how does one argue against another person's experience?

What is often really happening is that such a person has some sense of one or more past historical experiences by one or more ancestors. They may not have all of the details right, but there is, perhaps, some truth in what they sense. What they are experiencing is normal for people who are particularly sensitive to generational experiences. Unfortunately, without proper understanding, what they end up doing is misinterpreting what they are sensing. So, in order to make sense of what they feel, they assume that they had lived a previous life. In other words, they have a correct revelation (that something historical happened) but a wrong interpretation. In this case, they attribute it to reincarnation instead something generational.

This is just like the enemy: if he can't keep you from operating in your gifting, he will try to lead you astray in your application and interpretation. In some cases, reincarnation is the enemy's distraction from, and substitute for, correctly interpreting generational experiences. The enemy doesn't mind that you sense generational issues, but he sure doesn't want you to pray through generational iniquities. In addition, if he can, he will lead you astray by embellishing generational stories, adding details that never occurred.

Please note that not all instances of belief in past lives indicate that a person is actually sensing generational iniquity. Some people are being deceived outright, or they are simply ignorant, or they have a demon that has been passed down through the generations - it is familiar with the family history, and thus, is capable of transmitting accurate information about ancestors while twisting it at the same time. However, the possibility of a generational iniquity is definitely something to consider.

This is why we need to seek the Lord for insight and revelation and not to seek spirit guides and mediums. They will often confirm something that resonates as true. But, in the end, they will lead us astray, never dealing with root issues.

Question: *Aren't generational influences really demons trying influence us?*

In every instance in the Bible where the influence of generational iniquity is mentioned, demons are never stated as the reason for the problem or the influence. It is always the iniquity itself. It's important to realize that not all generational iniquities have demons associated with them. Yet, if, in some instances, there are demons associated with a generational iniquity, the demons are always the secondary problem.

Demons are an annoyance and a distraction. They are like flies attracted to garbage. If you shoo away the flies, you get relief, but it is often only temporary because the flies will come back. However, if you get rid of the garbage, then it is much easier to get rid of the flies. And, better yet, the flies won't come back.

Defilement is the garbage that attracts demons. This spiritual garbage consists of our unconfessed sins, transgressions and iniquities. Though not all garbage has flies, it still has the potential to attract them. Therefore, the more significant the defilement in our lives, the more likely it is to attract demons.

Demons would rather we focus on them, hoping that we won't discover, and deal with, the defilement. So, they try to draw the attention to themselves. Their primary goal is to tempt us to sin, thus producing more defilement. In some instances, they tempt us to respond as our ancestors had. So, the lies they speak are often based upon the negative decisions our ancestors had made, but they don't want you to know that. Such lies provide clues as to the nature of the generational iniquity.

Although we might assess their activities, we don't interview the demons, for they are liars. Instead, we bind them, meaning that we tell them, in Jesus' name, to shut up and cease their activities. Then, we ask the Lord to reveal the historical event(s) in which an iniquity was committed. Once the generational iniquity has been revealed and confessed, it's easy to get rid of the demons. Just command them to go in the name of Jesus.

Question: *What of Paul's warning, in I Timothy 1:4, against giving heed to endless genealogies?*

In the surrounding verses, Paul is speaking of faith as opposed to false doctrines (as does Titus 3:9). One such false doctrine is when a person attempts to establish his or her salvation and righteousness on anything other than faith. Our identity as Christians isn't because of our pedigree, and this is what Paul was arguing against. Essentially, he was saying that we don't establish ourselves, or gain some sort of spiritual status, just because we can prove that we descended from certain godly people. John the Baptist confronted the Pharisees and Sadducees about this very matter (Matthew 3:7-9). Our faith is simply in Christ and what He did on the Cross. Even Paul, who had a tremendous spiritual and religious heritage, said, "But what things were gain to me, those I counted loss for Christ." (Philippians 3:5-7)

So, we aren't to dwell on genealogies to establish our righteousness and good standing before God. As it says in Titus 3:4-7:

> But when the kindness of God our Savior and His love for mankind appeared, He saved us, not on the basis of deeds which we have done in righteousness, but according to His mercy, by the washing of regeneration and renewing by the Holy Spirit, whom He poured out upon us richly through Jesus Christ our Savior, so that being justified by His grace we would be made heirs according to the hope of eternal life.

While we are not saved or righteous because of our ancestors in our genealogy, we can study our family line to know our family history, so as to identify generational iniquities and blessings. In addition, God included genealogies in the Bible for our encouragement and edification, so that we might learn from the failures and victories of the lives of others.

Generational Influence Potential

God blessed them; and God said to them,
"Be fruitful and multiply, and fill the earth..."
Genesis 1:28

The potential of generational influence is very significant!
Not only do we inherit from our ancestors, but we also leave an
inheritance for our descendants.

The following provides an approximation of generational
populations. Though this doesn't take intermarriage or the
occasional end of a family line into consideration, it does
illustrate the power of exponential growth. Though it doesn't
include adoption and stepparents, these do bring influence as
well.

Potential Influence upon One's Descendants

The following formula may be used for calculating the
cumulative number of people related to one person after a
specific number of generations. This represents the total
number of people who will be potentially influenced by one
person's life, generationally.

$$\text{Total} = N \cdot \frac{(1 - N^G)}{(1 - N)}$$

Total = the cumulative number of people
N = the average number of children per family
G = the number of generations from an individual

For instance, if a couple had two children, those two
children will inherit any influences from their parents. If each
child becomes an adult and has two children, that makes four
grandchildren. Thus, any influences from the original couple
are passed on to six individuals - the two children plus the four
grandchildren. As you can see, the numbers grow exponentially

with each subsequent generation. If each generation has an average of three children, it grows even faster. See chart.

Generational Totals Chart			
G	N = 2	N = 3	N = 4
1	2	3	4
2	6	12	20
3	14	39	84
4	30	120	340
5	62	363	1,364
6	126	1,092	5,460
7	254	3,279	21,844
8	510	9,840	87,380
9	1,022	29,523	349,524
10	2,046	88,572	1,398,100
11	4,094	265,719	5,592,404
12	8,190	797,160	22,369,620

If each descendant has an average of three children, then, in five generations, there will be cumulative total of 363 descendants. In eight generations, the total will be 3,840 descendants! Below is a graph of the above numbers, demonstrating the exponential nature of generational influence.

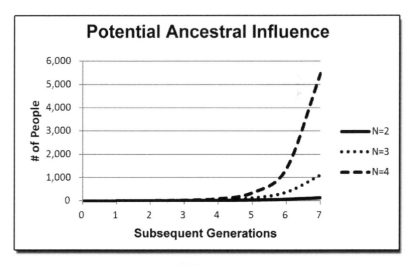

Potential Influence Coming from One's Ancestors

The same formula can be used for calculating the cumulative number of ancestors in a given number of generations. This is done by setting N = 2, since every child originates genetically from two parents. So, going back ten generations, one has a potential of 2,046 parental influences!

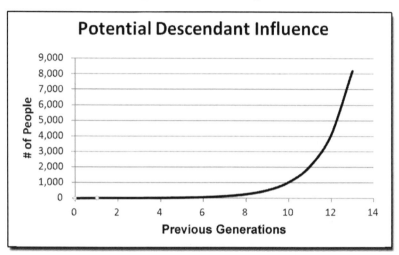

The above information illustrates the huge potential that both godly character and iniquities have within a family line. We are so blessed that the Lord has provided a means to put a stop to generational iniquity. And, in addition to the blessing we can receive, we can also bless our descendants by sowing godly character through obedience, endurance, prayer and self-sacrifice.

So, my encouragement to you is to:
- Deal with all of your known personal iniquities.
- Pray through all of the generational iniquities that God reveals to you.
- And sow godly character into your life so subsequent generations may be all the more blessed!

Genealogies in the Bible

A genealogy contains a list of names, consisting of individuals who are related to each other by blood or adoption. There are many such genealogies listed in the Bible.

As shared in this book, insights can often be found when studying genealogies in the Bible. They are more than just lists of who begat whom. Below is a list of genealogies in the Bible. By studying them, you are sure to discover additional insights.

Genesis 4:17-26; 5:3-32; 10:1-32; 11:10-32; 19:36-38; 22:20-24; 25:1-4; 35:22-26; 36:1-43; 46:8-27
Exodus 6:14-25; 35:30-34
Leviticus 38:21-23
Numbers 1:4-43; 2:3-32; 3:1-4; 3:17-35; 13:4-15; 16:1; 26:5-61; 27:1; 34:19-28
Ruth 4:13-22
I Samuel 1:1-2; 9:1-2; 14:49-52
II Samuel 3:2-5; 8:16-18; 23:24-39
I Kings 4:1-19
I Chronicles 1-9; 11:26-47; 12:3-7; 14:3-4; 15:4-10, 17-24; 23:7-23; 24:20-30; 26:1-32; 27:1-34
II Chronicles 11:18-23
Ezra 2:1-62; 7:1-5; 8:1-14; 10:18-44
Nehemiah 7:6-64; 10:1-27; 11:4-36; 12:1-26; 32-36
Matthew 1:1-17
Luke 3:23-37

How to Become a Christian

If you desire to become a Christian, pray the following prayer to Jesus.

"Jesus, I acknowledge that I am a sinner and that You died for my sins. I receive You as my Lord and Savior. Come into my life. I ask that you fill me with your Holy Spirit and that You direct me in all that I do."

Congratulations! You are now God's child.

Now that you have become a Christian, do the following:
- Find another Christian, and tell him/her what you did today!
- Get involved in a local church, especially one that has small home-groups during the week, which meet for Bible study and prayer.
- Begin reading the Bible. I encourage you to begin with the New Testament, starting with book of John.
- Spend time with Jesus in prayer. He has loves spending time with you!

31886861R00094

Made in the USA
San Bernardino, CA
22 March 2016